Napoleon Hill's
CAREER SUCCESS PLAN

Napoleon Hill's

CAREER
SUCCESS
PLAN

MASTERING THE MINDSET — FOR — ACHIEVEMENT —

THE NAPOLEON HILL FOUNDATION

Published and distributed by:
SOUND WISDOM
P.O. Box 310
Shippensburg, PA 17257-0310

717-530-2122

info@soundwisdom.com

www.soundwisdom.com

While efforts have been made to verify information contained in this publication, neither the author nor the publisher assumes any responsibility for errors, inaccuracies, or omissions. While this publication is chock-full of useful, practical information; it is not intended to be legal or accounting advice. All readers are advised to seek competent lawyers and accountants to follow laws and regulations that may apply to specific situations. The reader of this publication assumes responsibility for the use of the information. The author and publisher assume no responsibility or liability whatsoever on the behalf of the reader of this publication.

ISBN 13 TP: 978-1-64095-539-4

ISBN 13 eBook: 978-1-64095-540-0

For Worldwide Distribution, Printed in the U.S.A.

1 2 3 4 5 6 7 8 / 29 28 27 26 25

CONTENTS

INTRODUCTION

by
Don M. Green

Napoleon Hill was born in the rugged mountains of Southwest Virginia; and at the time, it seemed that his life would look like the lives of men in the area. Education was limited and school was not mandatory. Few adults saw the benefit of an education since they spent their days laboring in the coal mines. When boys turned 14, they would work as much as 14 hours a day in the underground coal mines. Most were paid very little and the work was extremely laborious. In addition, coal mining was dangerous. In fact, it was considered one of the most dangerous professions in the United States.

Napoleon's mother, Sara, died when she was 24 and Napoleon was only 9 years old. The future looked bleak for Napoleon, and it seemed that he was headed straight for the coal mines. However, all of that changed when Napoleon's father married a young widow named Martha Ramey Banner. Martha had previously been married to a school principal and was the daughter of a local physician. In other words, Martha's background was drastically different from that of young Napoleon. Martha quickly noticed that her stepson was drifting, so she began working with him in order to change his mindset. Martha provided encouragement to her stepson and bought him his first typewriter—a gift that changed the course of Napoleon's life.

Martha passed away in 1941, but she lived long enough to see Napoleon achieve success. She was able to read his magazines and his famous books: *Law of Success, Magic Ladder to Success, Think and Grow Rich,* and *How to Sell Your Way Through Life.* She supported him even when many others felt he was crazy for devoting his life to the success principles.

Many felt he was wasting his time by interviewing Andrew Carnegie in 1908. However, that interview with Andrew Carnegie started a 20-year journey that led to the development of a success philosophy that has helped millions achieve the life of their dreams. Today, people worldwide have benefited from Napoleon Hill's work that all started with a little encouragement from his stepmother.

SECTION ONE

THINK AND GROW RICH

PRINCIPLES

1

DOMINATING DESIRE

Desire is the starting point of all achievements.

Many people are half-hearted about our deepest desires. The most outstanding revelation of our time—that human beings can change their lives by changing their thoughts—requires that we possess a burning desire directed toward a primary definite purpose. This desire must be strong—to the point of obsession—until the goal or object is achieved.

MAKE YOUR DREAMS REALITY

Desire must be directed at both thought and the daily actions necessary to make your dream a reality. The following instructions are the means to develop a positive mental attitude that attracts to you the things and the people related to your aims and purposes in life.

Number one: Draw a clear picture in your mind of precisely what you desire and begin to live and act as you would if the desire had already been realized. Back your desires with as many basic motives as possible. *Keep your desires active at all times through both physical and mental action.* Inactivity in regard to desires is worthless.

Number two: Sell yourself into believing you will have the objects of your desires. Keep your mind off of circumstances and things you do *not* desire, because the mind attracts what it feeds on. Believe you are entitled to realize the objects of your desires, including what you intend to give in return—and start giving where you stand. Form the habit of obtaining information essential for getting your desires by asking questions of people who have the right answers.

Number three: Keep the object of your desires to yourself, lest you set up jealousy and oppositions that may defeat you. Place as many people as possible under obligation to you by the habit of going the extra mile in rendering more service than what is expected of you.

Number four: Keep your mind free of envy and anger and greed and hatred and jealousy and revenge and fear because these are the seven dark winters of failure.

Later, you will read about how to develop a positive mental attitude and use faith in your own personal success story. Before we go on to look into your primary purpose, we need to check out other related topics.

CHOOSE YOUR CAREER INTELLIGENTLY

If you are just starting out in search of your first position, you may opt to accept whatever employment you can get so you can earn a living while gathering the information you need to make your choice of occupation intelligently. Should you do this, be sure to regard the job as *temporary*. If you become indifferent about your life work or remain at your temporary job from force of habit or because you lack the power of decision to choose a more suitable position, you will never achieve success.

DO THE NEXT THING

You may not have any idea what kind of position to look for to fulfill your dominating desire. Or you may feel that you have no options at this point in your life.

No matter how bleak your opportunity picture may appear to be, there is usually one or more ways you can go; one or more options to choose from. If only one door seems to be open to you, enter it. Take a step into that career future. Don't just sit and wait for something to happen or for good fortune to come your way. *Do the next thing.*

Many times in your life, there will be periods when you feel stymied or when there is no hope on the horizon. But if you give your situation and your options some serious thought, and communicate with others in your dilemma through the Master Mind Mandate principle of success, you will discover that in fact there is a direction open to you.

This is when you must decide to do the next thing. That may be a decision to take a job that you know is open to you, even though you don't believe it's the answer to your life's quest for the right job or vocation.

Rather than sit around waiting for the right job, take the one at hand. It will very likely lead you to another position, a better one. That next job also may not be your idea of "job heaven," but it will very likely lead you to another opportunity.

Often we find our life's work in a circuitous way. Seldom is there a short, direct path to job or career success; the road may long and wide, but if we stay active and positive in our thoughts that a brighter future is ahead if we work toward it, we will reach the heights we set our minds to.

Inactivity is the cousin of the twins of indecision and procrastination. Kill off the failure factor of inactivity by remembering that when there seems to be no way to turn or no opportunity ahead, just do the next thing.

LIKE WHAT YOU DO

It's pathetic to see people who have committed themselves to a wearisome treadmill of toil for their entire lives, spending five or six days a week at work they don't like. Such people have sentenced themselves to a prison term approximating five- or six-sevenths of their entire life.

The reason you should choose an occupation you like is obvious. If you enjoy your work, it never becomes burdensome or tiring. People get tired not from overwork, but from a lack of interest in what they're doing.

If you not only like what you're doing, but have a desire and passion for it, you are on your way to a life of pleasure where your work and rewards may be hard to imagine right now.

How can you avoid doing work you don't like? By deciding not to become a prisoner for life in a prison of your own making. Or if you find yourself temporarily in such a prison because of the necessity of earning a living, you can release yourself by deciding that you're going to select another occupation and then follow that decision with action in harmony with the instructions described in this book.

We are all creatures of habit!

We are *where* we are and *what* we are because of our habits of thought and action. But we don't have to remain victims of these habits. We can change our habits—and consequently change our life's circumstances.

SOMETHING FOR NOTHING

Life has no bargain counters. Everything has a price that must be paid in one form or another.

The price of success in marketing your personal services is measured in a great variety of terms and equivalents, all of which are plainly described in this book. Familiarize yourself with these price tags and decide if you are willing to pay the price.

If you are reading this book in the hope that it may explain some plan of "hocus-pocus" by which you sell your services for more than they are worth, lay the book down right now. On the other hand, if you want money in greater quantities than you are now receiving and are prepared to give in return an equivalent of service, this book will guide you safely over the pitfalls and mistakes that even the most sincere people sometimes make.

This is an age when the predominating tendency of people is to get without giving. That tendency toward avarice and greed is in the very air; and if you don't watch yourself, you will become a victim yourself.

I emphasize this danger for the benefit of young people who are not yet victims of this mad desire for something for nothing. I qualify my statement to apply to young men and women, because I know that only a few of the older ones, whose habits have become so fixed, will pay any attention to this warning.

Many young people think they can become rich and famous entertainers, sports or movie or TV stars, but few of them know how hard they have to work to achieve what others have. No great and wealthy athlete or entertainer achieved fame and fortune without putting in long hours, days, and years of learning their sport or craft. There are no such things in the superstar world as "overnight successes." Every star who earns the adulation of millions and paychecks of the same size got to the top of his or her profession through having a dominating desire, hard work, practice, positive attitudes, and by applying the other principles of vocational and life success found in this book.

Once in a very great while, life picks up someone off the sidewalk and gives the person what might be called instant success. But nature has a way of balancing the books. If that person has not been properly prepared for success, it will quickly be gone. Those who have been fortunate enough to acquire temporary possession of something they have not paid full value for are at one time or another forced to surrender it.

This rule applies to the delivery of personal services as well as all other transactions. You might get by for a time by rendering, or providing, services that are inadequate in quality and quantity, but nature's auditor will be waiting just around the corner.

This book was not written with the purpose of describing how easy it is to receive big money by rendering inadequate service. Its purpose is to describe definite ways of earning money by rendering its equivalent in satisfactory service.

FITTED BY DESIRE

Before determining what position or calling you desire, decide whether you merely want a position, or the position you are best fitted for by desire, education, and native ability.

Check out personality tests online, ask trusted friends and family for feedback on what they see as your strengths and weaknesses, etc.—at work, in relationships, motivation, and the like. Personality assessments predict success, determine job fitness, and provide accurate insights regarding a person's strengths, weaknesses, and preferences.

The next decision is to determine whether you prefer a position that offers great opportunity in the future with modest pay at the start, or one that yields the maximum amount of pay, but offers no promise for the future.

In other words, you must decide whether you want to start at the top or at the bottom of the ladder. Don't make the mistake of thinking that is an obvious decision. Starting at the top can prove to be a bad career decision, while working your way up from a lower position may be the smartest way to reach the top. This decision determines to a large extent the ultimate amount of your earning capacity, since it is obvious that someone who starts at the top can move in only one direction.

FACTORS IN CHOOSING YOUR OCCUPATION

When considering your dominating desire, you must make five decisions before you can create a plan for marketing yourself and the services you have to offer:

1. Decide which calling or occupation you like best. Careful analysis of many thousands of men and women has shown that people experience the greatest and most enduring success when engaged in the kind of work they like best.

2. Decide what type of employer you prefer. It is just as important for you to choose your employer with care as it is for an employer to choose his or her employees with care. Pick a boss you have confidence in and whose conduct is most valuable to you. Remember too that your boss will be your teacher, so make sure your teacher is capable.

3. Decide how much money you intend to earn for the first five years. Remember that the amount of your annual earnings is the equivalent of one-sixth of the capital value of your brain. If your income is $25,000 a year, your brain capital is the equivalent of $150,000. Regard this capital as something you must keep working if you are to collect the income.

4. Decide—the most important decision—*exactly the quality and the quantity of service you intend to deliver in return for the income you expect to demand, and deliver at least that much!* Most people devote more time to thinking about the money they want or need than they do to creating ways and means of earning that amount through an equivalent service.

5. Decide if you are stymied by any major causes of failure (see Chapter 4) *and select an occupation that eliminates or at least minimizes that deterrent.*

These five decisions are some of the most important you will ever have to make. Reach them promptly, but with due thought and deliberation, because your whole future depends on the decisions you make.

Before you even start to negotiate for a readjustment of your salary if you are presently employed or seek employment elsewhere, be sure you are worth more than you now receive.

It is one thing to *want* more money, but it is entirely different to be *worth* more! Many people mistake their wants for their "just dues."

Your financial requirements or wants have nothing whatever to do with your worth. Your value is established entirely by your ability to render useful service or your capacity to induce others to render such service.

LABOR'S ROMANCE

I am, by nature, an optimist. I would not rob labor of its romance, if I could do so. To me, there is nothing more romantic in life than a person and a job that are suited to each other. If life offers anything that will bring more happiness than the privilege of rendering useful service that someone enjoys, I don't know what it is.

Millions of people lack employment and other millions realize from their labor barely enough for existence. Out of this experience have come many helpful lessons, among them the sure knowledge that there is one thing worse than being forced to work—being forced *not* to work.

No one can be happy without some form of occupation. Many have tried to find happiness in pleasure and have failed. Enduring happiness comes through serving. All other forms of happiness are transitory and delusive.

HAPPINESS COMES FROM *ASPIRING,* NOT FROM *ACQUIRING*

I have known scores of people of great wealth. Without exception, those who had a dominating desire found their happiness not in the millions of dollars they acquired, but from aiming, hoping, creating, and building plans for future achievement.

You, too, can find happiness through your efforts if you learn how to market your personal services effectively. This book shows you how to do that.

TAKE ACTION NOW

Get started *now* to identify your dominating desire and then develop a master plan for your career and life. The following are a few ways you can begin:

1. Make a list of things you like to do. Underscore those you have the most knowledge of. Double underscore the things that give you pleasure *and* desire *and* can bring you financial rewards.

2. Mentally prepare yourself to accept both life's joys and its bitterness. Make up your mind that any failure will be only a temporary condition.

3. Write down on a sheet of paper your responses to the five decisions you are asked to make in choosing your occupation. Ask your spouse, trusted friend, parents, favorite teacher, or counselor to go over the list with you and help

you to make wise and decisive decisions to the five factors.

4. Read the 31 major causes of failure in Chapter 4 and circle the ones that may apply to you. Start now to eliminate those roadblocks from your path to success.

5. If you can't see any road ahead to take, assess what directions there are. If you see only one way ahead, go that route.

6. Do the next thing. It may not be the perfect job or solution to your problem, but it can lead to other opportunities that can bring you success, wealth, and happiness.

7. Make a list of the most successful men and/or women you know or admire. Ask yourself what made them rich and famous. Do you desire to follow any of them in their chosen profession?

8. What are your desires, hopes, dreams, ambitions? If you don't have any, now is the best time to start discovering them. Only with a primary purpose, or main aim in life, a goal to shoot for, can you create a master plan to achieve what you want in your life.

In *Think and Grow Rich,* I tell the story of Edwin C. Barnes and how his dominating desire to become associated with Thomas Edison led to his success.

Barnes was a struggling young man who had a burning desire to work for the famous inventor. But he had two strong marks against him from the start. First, he didn't know Edison or know anyone who could introduce him to the great man. Second, he didn't even have the train fare to get to Edison's laboratory in East Orange, New Jersey.

These obstacles might have stopped a less-determined man, but they didn't stop Barnes.

He worked odd jobs until he earned the railway fare, then simply presented himself to Edison and announced he had come to go into business with the inventor.

Edison was not impressed with the young man's appearance since he wasn't wearing the suit of a successful person. But something did impress Edison enough to hire Barnes—the young man's determination. Edison told me later:

> There was something in the expression of his face which conveyed the impression that he was determined to get what he had come after. I had learned, from years of experience with men, that when a man really desires a thing so deeply that he is willing to stake his entire future on a single turn of the wheel in order to get it, he is sure to win.

Edison gave Barnes the opportunity he wanted because he could see that the young man had made up his mind to stand by until he succeeded. He hired Barnes at a very nominal wage and set him to work in the Edison offices. It wasn't instant important work, but Barnes got what he wanted, a start with the great inventor. He had enough determination to work that humble first job into something of much greater importance.

Months went by and Barnes still waited for his big break. He kept telling himself to be patient and persevere, to do his best work, and when his big opportunity would come, he would be ready for it.

As often happens, Barnes's opportunity came in a way he had not planned for. This is one of the tricks of opportunity. It has a sly habit of slipping in by the back door, and often comes disguised as misfortune or temporary defeat. This may be why so many people fail to recognize opportunity.

Edison had just perfected a new office device that he called the Edison Dictating Machine, but his salesmen weren't enthusiastic about it. Barnes thought differently. He familiarized himself with the machine and developed a great confidence in it. Then he told Edison he knew he could sell it.

Edison gave Barnes a chance to prove his conviction about the machine and Barnes realized this was the chance he had been waiting for and dreaming of. He put everything he had into his effort to promote and sell the dictating machine and became so successful at it that Edison gave him a contract to distribute and market it nationwide. Barnes soon grew rich and realized his great ambition. Now he was working not *for* but *with* the great inventor.

Barnes had literally *thought* himself into a partnership with the great Thomas Edison. He persevered until he got a job with him, then worked so hard he was ready when opportunity came.

He had nothing to start with except the capacity to know what he wanted in life, then developed the determination to stand by his goal until he achieved the success he desired.

My friend and colleague W. Clement Stone agrees with me that *success is a journey, not a destination.*

A career, great wealth, and business are worthy goals to set in life. For many, they may be enough.

But for the greatest achievers, those goals are not enough. Men such as Ford, Edison, Carnegie, and Stone set even higher goals for themselves, goals that reached beyond material success. Their dominating desire inspired them to be of help and service to others, and once they acquired great wealth, they gave away much of their financial resources to benefit humankind. An altruistic primary definite purpose is such a higher goal that it can ascend the heights of the human spirit.

Don't be afraid to aim high in choosing your life goal, for the higher it is, the more room you will have for achievement.

TWO DOMINATE DESIRE SUCCESS STORIES

Scott Fletcher
Million-Dollar Ballplayer

Scott "Scooter" Fletcher is the only player in MLB history to play for the Cubs, White Sox, Tigers, and Brewers.

He played shortstop so well, that the Texas Rangers signed him to a three-year, $3.9 million contract. Not bad, $1.3 million a year for a young man who went 600 at-bats without hitting a single home run, and stole bases 33 times in three years but got caught 28 times.

At the age of 30, Fletcher became one of the most sought-after shortstops in the American League at a time when good shortstops were in short supply. His manager said Scooter was in the right place at the right time, with the right marketing commodity.

But, like many other superstars, Fletcher's was not a case of an overnight success. He broke into the majors with the Chicago Cubs in 1981 and got traded to the White Sox two years later. It was a slow, unpromising start for a boy from Wadsworth, Ohio, where his father taught physical education and coached high school baseball and football. Fletcher made up his mind early, when he was only 13, that he wanted to become a professional ballplayer. While other kids were lazing in the sand at the beach or going to parties, Scooter was at the school diamond, practicing with friends or his older brother, Rick.

Fletcher worked on his batting, trying to regain the streak he had when he hit 17 home runs in one game as a Little Leaguer.

His father knew Scooter had it in him, not only to prove himself as one of the best shortstops in the game, but to swat more home runs and steal more bases. His faith in his son went back to the cold January day when Scooter and his brother were teenagers, leaving the warm house to go out and play a game of toss against the back fence, the temperature outside only 14 degrees. Neighbors walked by thinking the boys were crazy, but Scooter told them he had to get ready for the start of the baseball season that spring.

That's what I mean by a primary desire. Scott Fletcher had made up his mind that he wanted to be a great baseball player, and he worked at it until he became one, and a millionaire several times over, besides.

Michael Jordan
Basketball Superstar

A factory worker's son from North Carolina grows up to become a basketball superstar earning millions of dollars a year. A miracle that could only happen in the United States of America, and only because of high motivation and success goals set early in life.

Michael Jordan, Chicago Bulls basketball star and National Basketball Association champion, was born to working-class parents in Brooklyn who later settled in Wilmington, North Carolina. His father worked in a General Electric factory, and his mother was a customer relations supervisor at a bank. He became the third of five children in the family and had the good fortune of being surrounded by strong, loving parents who provided a positive home environment.

The Jordans taught their children early to make goals and work to achieve them. They were warned not to expect to get something for nothing in life, and not to sit around and wait for opportunity, but to make things happen. Delores Jordan gave Michael something extra—her competitive nature.

Growing up, Michael was faced with many temptations—traps like drugs and drink, which were easy to get on the streets. The Jordans warned against such traps and encouraged their children to exercise self-discipline if they hoped to be successful in life.

Michael turned his energies to Little League baseball and proved himself to be a good pitcher. But when he turned 13, he became more interested in basketball. His father, James, built a court in the backyard and Michael and his older brother, Larry, and their friends played basketball every day after school. Larry was taller than Michael then, and Michael had to play harder to compete against him. He became known as "Rabbit."

But basketball success did not come early for Michael. He failed to make the varsity team as a freshman in high school.

Trying harder and practicing longer, he made the varsity team in his sophomore year, but was cut early in the season. Yet Michael persevered. He worked even harder, practicing longer hours with his brother Larry.

While he waited to try again in his junior year, he worked on the track team, specializing in the long jump and high jump. When the basketball season rolled around again, Michael was ready for it.

The school's basketball coach, Clifton Herring, saw great potential in Michael and enrolled him in a basketball camp that gave him the boost in encouragement he needed. A burst of confidence soared through Michael and swept him on his way to greatness. With the help of his mentor, Coach Ferring, he went on to become first a college and then a pro superstar.

Michael Jordan says he owes his success to parents who gave him a lot of love and encouragement, a coach who saw his potential and helped him realize it, self-discipline that has kept him healthy both mentally and physically, and the perseverance to make his dreams come true.

As of spring 2024, Jordan's net worth is *$3.24 billion* from various enterprises and investments. He challenges other young people not to be like him, but to be better than him. That goal can be achieved through following Michael Jordan's positive path to success. It takes effort, determination, and telling yourself you can do anything you set your mind to. It takes setting a *definite desire* and *primary purpose*.

2

YOUR PRIMARY PURPOSE

**Success is not possible without
determining your primary purpose.**

People who know where they are going usually get there.
They don't waste their strength in aimless expenditure of time
and energy, following first one course and then another. Rather,
focused people concentrate their efforts on a definite objective,
exerting all powers toward that accomplishment.

Working with a desired primary purpose toward a single goal
has many advantages:

1. Singleness of purpose forces you to specialize,
    and specialization tends toward perfection.

2. A definite goal develops in you the capacity to
    reach decisions quickly and firmly.

3. A definite purpose overcomes the habit of
    procrastination.

4. A primary purpose saves time and energy
    otherwise wasted while wavering between two or
    more possible courses of action.

5. Singleness of purpose is a roadmap charting the direct route to the end of your journey.

6. A primary purpose overtakes your subconscious mind and uses it as a motivating force (involuntarily) to drive you toward your goal.

7. Definiteness of purpose develops your self-confidence and attracts other people's confidence in you.

SELECTING A DEFINITE MAIN AIM IN LIFE

You will never achieve outstanding success unless you have a definite major goal in life.

> # Definiteness of purpose is the starting point of all achievement.

In my hundreds of interviews with many of the great leaders and achievers of this country, I easily saw that having a primary purpose is their fundamental principle.

I also learned that 98 percent of the general public drifts aimlessly through life without the slightest idea of what work suits them best, and they had no conception whatsoever of the need to strive for a definite objective.

On the other hand, the 2 percent of the population who reach outstanding success did not settle for anything short of what they wanted from life.

The observation of thinking people over the centuries has been that a defined purpose is the starting point of achievement. It has been proven many times that if a person is really determined to get a thing, the person can get it.

If you have the ambition to start making life pay off on your own terms, you must have a definite goal in life. You must stimulate your thinking and awaken your desire for a primary purpose.

Your specific aim or ambition in life may result from different combinations of lesser or minor aims, including:

1. The nature of your occupation, which should be of your own choice, not one forced by another person.

2. The amount of your income, which should be sufficient for you to live at the standard of living you choose.

3. The budgeting of income and expenses to provide for sickness, accidents, or retirement.

4. A plan for developing and maintaining harmony in all of your human relationships: your personal and work life, where you play and relax. Human

relationships are vital to your aim in life—you must have people's cooperation to achieve any success above mediocrity.

5. The acquisition of material things, whether a house, car, boat, or the best audio-video equipment.

6. The love of someone special to you.

7. Service to others and contributing to the benefit of humankind.

Your objective, or some portion of it, should always remain a few jumps ahead of you, as something to look toward with hope and anticipation. The hope of achievement is one of the great riches of life.

Once you have achieved a substantial part of or all of your goal, a new, expanded, and widened purpose should be adopted. To test whether the objective you have in mind is worthy of being a specific goal in life, ask yourself: 1) Am I willing to spend most of my lifetime making it come true? 2) Will it be worth the price I may pay for it?

Don't hesitate to choose a definite goal that may, for the time being, be out of your reach. You can always prepare yourself by getting the qualifications you need for your objective. Always allow for personal growth and the development of your innate talent.

You may feel that you will never be completely ready to start any project that leads to reaching your major goal. There will always be something else you think you could do in preparation for your take-off. But if you *start where you stand and work with whatever tools you have at hand, other and better goals will reveal themselves as you move forward.*

When you adopt a primary purpose, a definite major purpose, you will see how quickly the habit of moving on your own personal initiative—proactive, self-starting behavior—will inspire you to act to achieve your purpose. Your imagination will become more alert, revealing to you myriad opportunities related to your purpose.

Opposition to your purpose will disappear, and people will give you their friendly cooperation.

Fear and doubt about the future will disappear also. And somewhere along the way, you will meet your "other self" face to face—the self who can and will carry you over into the success side of life.

From there on, the going will be easy and the way will be clear, for you will have adapted yourself to the great intangible forces of Nature that inevitably lead to the attainment of your chosen goal in life.

Then you will wonder why you hadn't discovered the path sooner; and you will understand why *success attracts more success*—while failure attracts only more failure.

SPECIFIC STEPS TO EMBRACE YOUR LIFE'S PRIMARY PURPOSE

First, take time to sit and think about what you really want out of life—for yourself, for others. What is your greatest aspiration? Your ultimate yearning? What brings a smile to your face every time it comes to your mind? Write down everything.

Then whittle down all those thoughts and write one clear statement that defines your primary purpose in life. When that is clear in your mind, next write a concise outline of the plan or plans to achieve the object of your purpose and the maximum time you intend to achieve it. Sign your statement and the plan, commit it to memory, and repeat it at least twice daily in the form of a prayer or affirmation. If you are married, have your mate sign the statement with you, and repeat it together just before retiring each night.

Next, describe in detail precisely what you intend to give in return for the realization of your purpose, keeping in mind that everything has a price that must be paid. Keep your definite major purpose strictly to yourself and your mate, if married. Call your primary purpose into your conscious mind as often as practical. Eat with it, sleep with it, and take it with you every hour of the day. Keep in mind that your subconscious mind can even be influenced to work toward your goal while you sleep.

THE JUNK DEALER

The following is a very interesting case that shows what may happen when people neglect to move forward in life without a primary purpose.

R.U. Darby from Baltimore, Maryland, had the good fortune to discover a very rich vein of gold while vacationing in the West. He returned home and borrowed money from friends and relatives to install mining machinery and went to work mining the rich gold ore. All went well for a few weeks, then suddenly the vein stopped. In sheer desperation, Darby sold the mining equipment to a junk dealer for a fraction of what it had cost and he returned home.

The junk dealer proved himself smart by calling in a mining engineer who examined the mine, then announced that a fault in the earth had cut off the vein of ore. The junk dealer was told to keep digging and the vein would reappear. With a definite purpose, the junk dealer dug ahead just three feet, and picked up the vein again. His commitment to purpose yielded him several millions of dollars. The mine turned out to be one of the richest in the West.

Every day, men and women stop just short of a glorious success because they drift through life without aim or purpose. Let that not be you.

> ## Don't stop short of a glorious success.

At this point, I encourage you to stop reading and write out your definite primary purpose, your goal. Be sure to focus on specifics. List the information or knowledge you seek, the work you want to do, and or the kind of personality you desire. Write down what you want to be paid each year, the places you want to visit, the skills you want to possess, and give yourself a definite timetable in which to accomplish what you wrote.

When you're finished, make this statement a binding agreement, sign it, and think of it as an agreement with your subconscious. Your subconscious will work toward this purpose even when you aren't.

WRITE YOUR OWN SUCCESS STORY

You can write your own success story when you define your primary purpose, your definite major purpose, which includes implementing the following seven factors:

1. Know that the starting point of all achievement is the adoption of a *primary purpose* accompanied by a *precision plan* for its attainment followed by an *appropriate action.*

2. All individual achievements are the result of a *motive* or a combination of the following *nine basic motives:* love; sex; material wealth; self-preservation; freedom of body and mind; personal expression and recognition; perpetuation of life after death; revenge; fear.

3. *Any dominating desire,* idea, plan, or purpose is taken over by a stimulated subconscious mind and acted on through whatever natural and logical means available.

4. Any *precise plan* or purpose—backed by *follow-through faith*—is taken over by your subconscious mind and acted on almost immediately.

5. You have complete and unquestionable control over your *ingenious imagination* or *power of thought*.

6. The *master mind* appears to be the only doorway of individual approach to Infinite Intelligence. The basis of the approach is *faith* based on a definite purpose.

7. Determined *decision making* involves your *brain,* which is both a broadcasting set and a receiving station for thought.

An in-depth, comprehensive, and detailed explanation of a definite master purpose and these seven factors are found in my books: *Think and Grow Rich* as well as *Master Mind.*

Personal initiative is the power that starts all action!

Personal initiative is a prominent quality in fulfilling your primary purpose and a trait of all successful people in every field of endeavor, and includes:

- Motivation in continuous pursuit of your primary purpose.
- Personal energy and persistence to overcome

obstacles.

- An alliance with others to attain your definite purpose.
- Self-starting approach to goals and tasks.
- Self-reliance in proportion to the scope and object of your primary purpose.
- Self-discipline to ensure mastery of the head and the heart and to sustain your motives.
- Persistence, based on your will to win.
- A well-developed imagination, controlled and directed.
- The habit of reaching definite and prompt decisions.
- The habit of basing all opinions on known facts, not guesswork.
- The habit of "going the extra mile," doing more than you are expected to do.
- The capacity to generate enthusiasm at will and to control it.
- A well-developed sense of observation of details, large and small.
- The capacity to withstand criticism without resentment.
- Familiarity with the nine basic motives that inspire all human action.
- The capacity to concentrate your full attention on one task at a time.

- Willingness to accept full responsibility for subordinates' mistakes.
- The habit of recognizing the merits and abilities of others.
- A positive mental attitude at all times.
- The habit of assuming full responsibility for any job or task undertaken.
- The capacity for follow-through faith.
- Patience with subordinates and associates.
- The habit of following through with any task you begin.
- The habit of placing thoroughness ahead of speed.
- Dependability.
- The ability to recognize opportunities presented by every temporary defeat.

There are other qualities of minor importance that successful people require, but this is the *must* list of all future prosperous leaders. You can measure anyone with this list by observing how many of these traits apply—even if done so unconsciously.

Personal Initiative + Precise Plan + Definite Motive = Successful Career Life

To be effective, personal initiative must be based on a precise plan, inspired by a definite motive, and followed through to the end.

During World War II, Henry J. Kaiser astounded the entire industrial world by his achievements of speed and efficiency in building ships. His achievements were all the more amazing because he had never built ships before. The secret of his success was in his leadership ability.

The most *common cause of failure is the habit of drifting* through life without a primary purpose. People with personal initiative do not drift; they do not procrastinate; they do not complain of the lack of opportunity—*they move on their own responsibility* and create opportunities for themselves!

DEFINITE PURPOSE

A definite purpose sparked W. Clement Stone who had a single burning desire to build a large insurance company.

When Stone was three, his father died; and at the age of six, he started his work life by delivering newspapers. His mother found work as a dressmaker. When he was 13, Stone ran a newsstand of his own and devoured rags-to-riches books of Horatio Alger.

When Stone was 16, he moved from Chicago to Detroit where his mother had started an insurance agency. When school let out that summer, he joined his mother selling insurance and soon was earning $100 a week. With the great enthusiasm and positive mental attitude he later became famous for, Stone saw his future in sales and insurance, so he dropped out of high school to devote his full attention to insurance. Later, through night school, he earned a high school diploma and took university and law courses.

When he was 20, Stone used his savings of $100 to set up his own insurance agency in Chicago. It didn't take long before about a thousand agents were selling insurance for him. During the Great Depression of the 1930s, Stone expanded his business and effected mergers to build the Combined Insurance Company of America.

In 1937, Stone read my book *Think and Grow Rich,* which had just been published, and he later told me:

> I gained new insights from your book, and your philosophy for personal achievement coincided with my own in many respects. I thought my salesmen could benefit from the book, so I gave a copy of it to each of them and, Bingo! I hit the jackpot! Fantastic things began to happen!
>
> Many of my salesmen became supersalesmen. Sales and profits increased. Their attitude had changed from negative to positive. Those who were searching for the secret of success realized that they were important persons. They had unlimited potential powers to affect their subconscious minds through the conscious.

Within two years, Stone's insurance business became a huge success. Positive self-help thinking and motivation for success helped his business grow until he amassed a multimillion-dollar fortune.

In 1981, W. Clement Stone was nominated for the Nobel Peace Prize in recognition of his humanitarian work. He is one of the best examples of someone who developed a selfless primary purpose in life, then worked tirelessly to achieve his goal.

MAKE A MOVE

Move toward your goals on your own personal initiative, or personal ambition—no one will move for you. Begin now, right where you stand. Adopt a primary purpose, lay out a precise plan to reach it, and then take action on the plan. If the first plan doesn't work, change it for another, but you need *not* change your purpose.

You may not have all the material things you need to carry out your purpose, but take hope from the fact that as you make the best possible use of the materials you have, other and better materials will be made available to you—if you are ready to receive them and use them.

> **A prepared mind full of hope and a precise plan will attract opportunities.**

The mind that has been made ready to receive attracts what it needs, just as an electromagnet attracts steel filings. What greater opportunity, therefore, could you give to personal initiative than to condition your mind to attract what you need?

The most difficult part of any task is *starting*. But once started, opportunities and resources will present themselves. The truth of this has been proved by the fact that people with a primary purpose are more successful than those without an objective. There is no doubt that every successful person admits that having a primary purpose was the turning point of major lifetime importance.

No one can tell what someone else's definite primary purpose in life should be, but any successful person will verify the fact that success is not possible without such a purpose.

Outstanding examples of people who moved with a definite primary purpose expressed through personal initiative include:

- Christ, in moral precept and spiritual inspiration.
- Christopher Columbus, in exploration and navigation.
- Thomas A. Edison, in uncovering and harnessing natural laws; in the combination of the principles of science in new arrangements; in the field of invention.
- Guglielmo Marconi, in science and invention in the field of wireless communication.
- Walter P. Chrysler, production of popular priced, dependable automobiles.
- Mahatma Gandhi, in fighting illiteracy and superstition among his people in India.

- Napoleon Bonaparte, in military operations.
- Isaac Newton, in the study of natural laws, particularly the law of gravitation.
- Orville and Wilber Wright, in the early pioneering field of aeronautics.
- Abraham Lincoln, in preserving the unity of the United States of America.
- John D. Rockefeller, in industry and philanthropy.
- Louis Pasteur, in fighting physical diseases.
- Marie Curie, in discovering radioactivity and its medical applications.
- George Washington, in military operations and statesmanship.
- Benjamin Franklin, in statesmanship, business, philosophy and science.
- Alexander Graham Bell, in science and invention.

Always remember, action is the natural outgrowth of personal initiative, and action is a major fundamental of all personal achievements.

A PLUMBER'S PERSONAL INITIATIVE

In a southern city of about ten thousand people, lived a very plain type of man who gained both local fame and fortune because of his personal initiative.

Since this man had less than average ability and education, it is interesting to observe how he achieved noteworthy success in building a substantial business that has made him a man of more than ordinary financial means and influence in his community.

He didn't possess many talents that would naturally be associated with his distinctive achievements. As an employee of a plumbing establishment, he proved to be awkward, even clumsy, and obviously lacked the skill of the average pipefitter. Since he was unsatisfactory in the capacity of a plumber, his employer tried him out as a salesman, but he showed no promise whatsoever in this role.

Although he received no college training, he had finished high school and could write a clear, legible hand. Consequently, his employer decided he might make a satisfactory bookkeeper. But again, the results were discouraging to both his employer and himself.

However, during his bookkeeping experience, he realized perhaps for the first time *the necessity of taking inventory of himself.* He took time off from his job, went to a quiet place, and deliberately wrote out a list of the better qualities he knew he possessed:

1. The habit of saving money.

2. Ability to figure costs on a plumbing job, with accuracy.

3. Ability to recognize superior skill in others.

4. Persistence in sticking to any task assigned until finished.

5. Ability to induce others to work together in a spirit of harmony.

With this list of his good qualities, this mediocre plumber decided to exercise his own judgment, act on his own personal initiative, and launch a plumbing business of his own.

> **Self-Inventory: List your good qualities, decide to exercise your own judgment, act on your own personal initiative, and launch into a successful life.**

Using his meager savings, he rented a modest storeroom and had the name of his newly organized plumbing firm painted on the windows. Almost immediately, the best pipefitter employed by his former employer came to him and voluntarily asked for the privilege of working with him at whatever wages he could afford to pay.

Then the newcomer in the plumbing business looked around until he found a capable sales and contact person. He also employed a college student to do the bookkeeping on a part-time basis. With good judgment, he selected other needed personnel. As his business increased, he added other skilled workers to his staff.

Having chosen his helpers wisely, he proceeded with his primary purpose—to become the leading plumbing contractor in his city.

In a short time, he had large contracts for several new buildings. He carefully supervised all the work. In a few years, people throughout the county began to seek his services because he had established a reputation for high-quality service and reliability in the performance of his contracts.

With an eye for sound economy, he began to look around for ways to expand his plant and add to his equipment and supplies. Two miles outside of the city, he found a vacant hosiery mill building with a leaking roof and broken windows.

Moving cautiously, he inquired of the building owners what rent they wanted for it. A price was named, but it was a rather high price, the owner explaining that he would have to first spend a considerable amount on repairs.

The plumber countered with the suggestion that he be quoted the lowest possible price for the building as it stood without repairs. To his surprise, the figure named was less than he had expected to pay, and considerably less than he was paying for his building in the city.

He accepted the offer, put his staff to work on the building, replaced all broken glass, repaired the roof, and put the building in first-class condition. The owner of the building was so pleased with the improvements that he voluntarily gave the plumber a ten-year lease, at the low price rental fee that had been agreed on.

In less than ten years, the plumber had increased his business so greatly that he was in a position to buy the building.

Meanwhile, he had added skilled workers until he had the best organization in the plumbing business in his community.

There is nothing dramatic or unusual about this story, and that is precisely why I shared it with you. This plumber started with nothing but a definite primary purpose and a small amount of savings—but by exercising his self-generated plan, he built a paying business, step by step.

JUMP START

This is exactly the way most successful people who are in business have begun. They start in a humble capacity with few advantages, but the important point is that *they make the start on their own initiative.*

There is hardly a great industry to be found anywhere in the United States that didn't have its beginning in humble circumstances. Henry Ford, for example, began in a small, one-room brick building. Thomas A. Edison began under similar circumstances. But they *started!* That is the important thing to remember—make a start and do it single-handedly, under your own steam.

> # Personal initiative is born out of motive!

The Creator provided humankind with many ingenious methods of carrying out the divine plan for human advancement, not the least of which is what we are influenced by to do our best because of enticing motives that have been planted in our minds. The motives of love, sex, and the desire for economic security are the three most impelling of all the motives that inspire people to move independently.

The Creator provided that life on this earth will continue according to His plans, no matter what people may think they want, nor to what motives they may attribute the results of their personal initiative.

This is a fact well-known to every psychologist, but not everyone may recognize the possibility that behind all expressions of personal initiative is the Creator's plan to ensure our mental and spiritual growth through our own endeavors.

Two facts stand out like the sun in the heavens on a clear day:

1. The United States of America has grown to be the one of the most successful nations of the world, and has become known as the "cradle of freedom and human liberty" on a scale that has made it an example for all the world to observe and emulate.

2. The most outstanding feature of the American people as a whole is their well-known habit of moving on their own personal initiative.

And it has been no mere stroke of chance that blessed Americans with these two outstanding benefits that have provided unparalleled privileges of growth and progress. The privilege of having our own resourcefulness overshadows all other privileges we enjoy—this privilege of free enterprise through which the humblest people may choose their own motives and live their own lives and accumulate riches in whatever form and quantity they desire.

Motivated by their personal desire, purpose, and enthusiasm, leaders of American industry have given us the greatest industrial, engineering, and healthcare systems of the free world. These systems provide the major portion of all jobs, whether connected with industry or otherwise, and pays the major portion of all taxes for both state and federal governments.

> **The world needs you to act on your individual initiative, dominate desire, and primary purpose.**

The whole of what we call the American way of life is the accumulated riches, skills, and experiences of people who have taken action on their own ingenuity—their focus on their primary purpose made our nation what it is today. And what we need in the future, to make the most of this newborn age of opportunity, is more men and women with *creative vision, definite purpose,* and a *motive* to inspire them to move proactively on their individual initiative.

The changed world we have been forced to accept, through the circumstances of World Wars and the current turmoils, has so greatly multiplied our needs and our opportunities that we are now experiencing a shortage of leadership in almost every industry, business, and profession.

I have found that when you have a defined purpose, work becomes fun. You are motivated to pay the price and to do it cheerfully and willingly. You voluntarily study, think, and plan, building your enthusiasm and intensifying your burning desire to achieve your goals. While reaching toward your goal, you can ride out the setbacks and disappointments that may come along. When you are prepared for setbacks and disappointments, you can handle each one and sustain momentum.

Those who give up after experiencing setbacks or disappointments usually fail. They don't have the positive mental attitude to see setbacks and disappointments merely as *temporary* failures.

You may know about a young man who learned this great lesson of life. He became a millionaire, then lost the company he founded. But that experience didn't cause him to give up. He worked harder and came back to again ride the heights of success, this time higher than before. His name? Steve Jobs. He made his Apple, Inc. fortune in computers by identifying and focusing on a definite primary purpose.

Elon Musk is another entrepreneur who has made comebacks after setbacks. Born in South Africa, he moved to the United States seeking greater economic stability found only in America. After earning several college degrees, he founded numerous companies including his first, Zip2 in 1995 that he sold to Compaq for $307 million. He also founded Space Exploration Technologies (SpaceX) and designed Falcon rockets,

Dragon, and Starship. He is one of the major funders of Tesla, an electric car company. His is an eclectic, interesting, and intriguing succession of various careers. His net worth as of May 2024 equals $198 billion.

3

FOLLOW-THROUGH FAITH

Faith is the only known antidote to failure.

Follow-through faith, or applied faith, is called the dynamo of this science of personal achievement philosophy because it enables action. Faith is the state of mind where you relax your own reason and willpower to open yourself completely to the inflow of power from Infinite Intelligence.

When you apply faith, you accept guidance from Infinite Intelligence. Turning over problems to this guidance can be difficult until you realize that if you let it, the creative force of the entire universe can aid you in all your endeavors.

Faith is a mental attitude wherein the mind is cleared of all fears and doubts and directed toward attaining something definite through the aid of Infinite Intelligence. With faith, we can tap into and draw on the power of Infinite Intelligence at will. Faith is guidance from within, but nothing more. It will not bring you what you desire, but it will show you the path to travel to go after whatever you desire.

Faith acts through the brain cells of the subconscious mind, the subconscious acting as the gateway between the conscious mind and Infinite Intelligence. Keep that gateway open. Keep it free from self-imposed limitations—for Infinite Intelligence recognizes no such reality as limitations, except those imposed by an individual and those that call for a circumvention or a suspension of natural laws.

To apply your faith to success, you need to clear all doubts and fears from your mind, then direct your mind toward the attainment of something definite. If you allow it, help will follow.

Every person has the power to condition their mind for the expression of faith. Every person has this power, because every person has been provided by the Creator with complete control over his or her own mind. In fact, this is the only thing over which any person has complete control.

> **Thoughts of opulence and plenty bring prosperity—your mind attracts whatever your mind has been conditioned to attract.**

Here once more we are rubbing elbows with the supreme secret of all great achievements, and right here is an appropriate place to call attention to another great truth in connection with the power of the mind—namely, *the mind attracts what it dwells on.*

Thoughts of poverty and failure bring poverty and failure, just as sure as night follows day. And thoughts of opulence and plenty bring prosperity just as definitely. In other words, the mind attracts to us whatever our mind has been conditioned to attract.

The vast majority of people keep their minds trained on all the things they fear and do *not* want, including the fear of poverty, ill health, criticism, the loss of love and affection, and old age. These fears have a strange way of materializing.

People who have found the way to successful achievement keep their minds trained on the things they *do* want. And by their thinking, they condition their minds for the expression of that mysterious power known as faith.

Faith has been called the mainspring of the soul, through which our aims, desires, plans, and purposes may become reality. It sounds like an indefinite business, but there are some fundamentals you can use to build the power of faith.

EIGHT FAITH-BUILDING FUNDAMENTALS

1. Faith-building means having a primary purpose supported by personal initiative or action. There is no greater demonstration of the power of faith than to decide what you're going to do, to become determined in your own mind you're going to do it no matter how many things or how many people get in your way, how long it takes, or what you have to pay to do it. The power of faith allows you to form a definite plan and proceed where you stand to carry out that plan, whether the time is favorable or not. That's fundamental number one.

Don't be like the congregation who when the preacher announced that he was going to preach for rain come Sunday morning, and they all came to hear his marvelous sermon but nobody brought an umbrella. The preacher said to the congregation, "This is a heck of a fine audience. I'm going to preach on the procuring of rain, and nobody brings an umbrella. You might as well go home. Rain's not going to come if you don't believe it's coming." There's a lot in that statement. You have to learn to rely on your belief. For instance, if you start off wanting to make a million dollars and you don't have 10 cents, but you do have an objective and a plan for making it, you better make yourself believe you're going to make a million dollars, or chances are you won't.

2. Another fundamental of applied faith is to maintain a positive mind, *free from all negatives such as fear, envy, hatred, jealousy, and greed.* Remember that mental attitude determines the effectiveness of faith. And remember also that mental attitude is the only thing in this world that you have control over. That's an astounding and important factor in connection with this subject. When you get to the point where you recognize this truth and begin to apply it, you will change the entire affairs of your life. You can obtain your objectives with less effort than you ever did before, and you can remove all sources of worry and fear.

3. The next fundamental of faith is to develop and maintain a master mind alliance *with one or more people who radiate courage based on faith and are suited mentally and spiritually to carry out a given purpose.* The reason for building a master mind made up of people who are suited mentally and spiritually to your needs is because the people you associate with have a certain mental attitude that is contagious, and you are bound to pick it up, in spite of all you can do. If you associate every day with people who have perfect faith and a positive mind, you will have no trouble accomplishing what you start out to do. Oftentimes we're so close to our problems that it's a case of not being able to see the forest through the trees.

4. Recognize that every adversity carries an equivalent benefit, that temporary defeat is not failure until and unless it has been accepted as such. One of the most important aspects in maintaining applied faith is to recognize that no matter how many adversities you face, have faced, or ever will face in the future, and every heartbreak, throwback, failure, defeat, and adversity, no matter what its nature may be, it carries with it an equivalent benefit. If you are developing in your mind the power to use applied faith when these adversities or unpleasant circumstances come along, instead of groaning and mourning, instead of building inferiority complexes as a result, immediately start to look for an equivalent benefit.

Imagine having a nice house in the country, and you went out to the show one evening, leaving some very valuable diamond rings in the house. While you were gone, the house caught fire and burned down. When you returned home, you saw there was nothing but ashes, your home was destroyed. What is the first thing you would do? You'd start digging for the diamonds, wouldn't you? You'd start stirring around the ashes of adversity to find the one thing you could possibly redeem and bring out. I don't care what your defeat or challenge is—it carries with it an equivalent benefit. The Creator never allows anything to be taken away from anyone without providing in the same circumstance something of equivalent or greater value to take its place.

This applies to the death of your loved ones, which is perhaps the most tragic loss that you can imagine. But along with the loss of a loved one comes a potential possibility of a softened heart, of experiencing and doing something within yourself that you couldn't have done without that grief.

5. *The habit of affirming your definite major purpose in the form of a prayer at least once daily.* Affirm it in prayer or whatever form you please. If you have a certain ritual in connection with your religion that you use, use that. So long as you connect with what constitutes your primary purpose. Get in the habit of doing that. First thing you know, you'll get to thinking in terms of what you can do—and never think about what you can't do. If you want to do something badly enough, you can always do it.

One of my students asked me once, "What do you mean by 'badly enough'? What is badly enough?" I wonder if you have ever thought about the importance of being able to think or want something badly enough to be sure to get it. Well, that's wanting it so badly that no matter what else may happen, you're going to put everything you have in life into the fulfillment of that desire. Thinking about it, talking about it, seeing yourself already in possession of it. That's wanting something badly enough.

You must work yourself into a state of a burning desire; and when you do that and place that in back of a definite primary purpose, that constitutes one of the finest prayers in the world. The Creator will know what you want and that you have the right kind of mental attitude about it. If you go to prayer with the wrong kind of attitude, you remain empty-handed. No matter what form you pray in, you will always come back empty-handed unless your mental attitude backs up what you're going after. Unless you believe you're going to get it, unless you believe you're entitled to it, unless you're determined to get it, you won't get it.

6. A faith-building foundation of recognizing the existence of Infinite Intelligence. The individual is a minute expression of this intelligence. And as such, *the individual mind has no limitations except those accepted or set up in his or her mind.* I wish I could make that statement stronger—it's that important. If you follow this philosophy, you will prove to yourself that it is true. You have no limitations except those you have set up in your mind or permit the circumstances of life or the influence of other people to set up for you.

If you examine yourself carefully, you will find that the limitations that held you back in the past were largely the influences of other people. Very large. Maybe entirely the influences of other people. Or they have been due to the fact that you've been thinking in negative terms of fear. If you can rid yourself of negative influences, if you can rid yourself of all of those outside influences designed to break down your faith, the time will come when you can do anything you make up your mind to do.

7. Self-respect expressed through harmony with your own conscience. Unless you're on good terms with your own conscience, you will never make the fullest use of follow-through faith. The Creator very wisely set up for you a judge advocate to whom you can go to at all times to know what is right and what is wrong. There is no sane human being in this world who doesn't know at all times what is right and what is wrong, unless someone has choked off his or her own conscience and killed it by neglecting being guided by it. That will kill it all.

You have to be on good terms with your own conscience and let it be the dictator. There are times when you will have to make decisions as a result of your conscience that will be very unprofitable to you. Go ahead and make them without any hesitation. If your conscience doesn't back you up, don't do it. If your conscience backs you up, go ahead and do it. Don't ask anybody, because you don't need to ask anybody. That's why the conscience was given to you, to guide you, to ensure you make no mistakes. Those who kill off their relationship with their conscience sooner or later come into difficulty.

CREATE A FAVORABLE MENTAL ATTITUDE

To create a mental attitude favorable for the expression of faith, there are steps you need to take. And incidentally, your mental attitude is the lever, the pump handle, the valve through which you control your power of faith. As mentioned previously, your mental attitude is the only thing you actually control.

To create a mental attitude favorable for the expression of faith:

- First, you need to *know what you want* and determine what you have to give in return for it. Know what you want; that's step number one in creating a positive mental attitude, which is all there is in connection with follow-through faith.

- Next, when you *affirm the object* of your desires through prayer, let your imagination see yourself already in possession of it.

- Third, *keep your mind open* for guidance from within, and when you are inspired by hunches to move on some plan created by your imagination that leads in the direction of what you desire, accept the plan and act on it at once. Don't neglect the hunches you get. They're rich with opportunity, richer than you may think. Sometimes you may have a hunch that seems quite foolish because it leads you in a direction that you never thought you wanted to go—yet that's exactly what you needed.

- Remember always that there can be no such state of mind as faith without appropriate action. *Faith without deeds is dead.* Action—there must be eternal action behind what you go after if you're going to make use of follow-through faith.

- And next, when overtaken by defeat, as you may be many times, remember that faith is tested many times, and defeat may be only one of your testing times. Don't accept it as anything else. Therefore, accept defeat as the inspiration for greater effort and carry on with belief that you will succeed. If you believe, you deserve to succeed.

- And last, any negative state of mind will destroy the power of faith and result in a negative climate. Your state of mind is everything, and you alone control your state of mind. There may be times when circumstances will make it difficult for you to control your state of mind, such as the death of a loved one. During those times, it will be very difficult for you to control your emotions, to not feel the pangs of sorrow. But if you practice controlling your state of mind, you will get to the point where you can control your mental attitude at all times to be positive.

There are two types of circumstances people worry about that destroy the power of faith. One is when you can do something about the situation if you wish to—and the other is when you have no control of the situation. Obviously the latter should be dismissed from your mind entirely because you can do nothing about it. You can relate yourself to those circumstances in such a way that they do not take you down. But the kind you can do something about—instead of worrying and becoming afraid and destroying your capacity for faith—that's when you jump in and *do* something, take control.

8. The faith-building fundamental of a burning desire— when faith is created. When you lay out a definite primary purpose and have a burning desire to fulfill that purpose, do not back away from it. Bring it into your consciousness many times a day and determine to carry out that purpose, which constitutes the finest application of faith you can imagine.

BUILD YOUR SELF-CONFIDENCE

You won't believe in an Infinite Intelligence if you don't believe in yourself. So now we look at eight steps to build your self-confidence, your faith in yourself, and your faith in the world at large.

1. Adopt a definite primary purpose and begin at once to attain it, using the instructions in this book.

2. Associate your primary purpose with as many as possible of the nine basic motives (cited in Chapter 2 and expanded on in Chapter 9).

3. Write a list of all the benefits and advantages that your definite major purpose would give you, and call these into your mind many times daily, thereby making your mind success-conscious through subconscious stimulation.

4. Associate as closely as possible with people who are in agreement with you and the object of your major purpose; seek their encouragement. This is referring only to your close friends or master mind associates (see Chapter 7).

5. Let not a single day pass without making at least one definite move toward fulfilling your definite primary purpose. Your daily watch word must be action, action, and more action.

6. Choose some prosperous, self-reliant person as your pacemaker, and make up your mind not only to catch up with that person, but to pass him or her with your own achievements. Do this silently without disclosing your plans to anyone.

7. Surround yourself with inspirational books. Pictures, wall-posted mottos, and other suggestive evidences of self-reliance, as demonstrated by other people. Build an atmosphere of achievement around yourself.

8. Adopt the policy of never running away from disagreeable circumstances; rather, stand your ground and fight it out until you overcome. Give no thought whatsoever to procrastination, as it may become an inferiority complex.

A properly conditioned mind accepts temporary defeat only as an urge to greater action, and thereby throws itself in the lap of the power that operates this universe. When I began publishing the *Golden Rule* magazine many years ago—without operating capital but with full belief I could make it pay—I uttered a prayer of the highest order. The magazine earned more than $3,000 the first year.

I didn't learn until ten years later, in a conversation with publishing magnate Bernard Macfadden, that to start a national magazine with any assurance of making it a success, a person must have $1 million in capital. How fortunate I didn't know this in advance! By properly conditioning my mind, I went ahead with my desire to publish the magazine in precisely the same way I would have proceeded if I had had the million dollars in the bank to begin with.

Once you've seen the power of true faith in action, it will be difficult for you to ever doubt it again.

HARNESSING THE POWER OF FAITH

Silent meditation or prayer are powerful tools for harnessing the power of faith. People worldwide have stories of miracles large and small that they believe came as a result of their faith and prayers. One of those miracles was revealed when our second son, Blair, was born, and we put our follow-through faith to work.

When Blair came into the world, he arrived without any ears, no sign of ears. The two doctors, his mother's uncles, who brought him into the world met me in the rotunda of the hospital, hoping to soften the shock I would undergo when I saw my son. They explained that there had been a few other children known to medical science born under similar circumstances, and they wanted me to know in advance that not one of them ever learned to hear or to speak. They wanted me to realize that my son would be a deaf-mute, as was the phrase during that time.

Well, that's as far as they got. I stopped them right then and said, "Now listen, doctors, I haven't seen my son yet, but I can tell you this. He will not be a deaf-mute, and he'll go through life with 100 percent of his hearing, just like all normal children."

The other doctor who hadn't been talking came over and put his hands on my shoulders and said, "Now look here, Napoleon. There are some things in this world that neither you, nor I, nor anyone else can do anything about, and you might just as well recognize that you are facing one of those circumstances."

I said, "Doctor, there isn't anything in this world that I can't do something about. If it's nothing more than adjusting myself to an unpleasant circumstance so my heart doesn't break, I can do that."

And I started immediately to do just that. I made up my mind before I saw my son that under no circumstances was I going to accept him as a child who couldn't hear or speak. Under no circumstances was I going to accept his condition as an affliction. Under no circumstances was I going to stop until he had 100 percent of his hearing. I had no idea how it was going to come about. The only thing I was sure about was that it was going to happen.

When you go at anything with that attitude, you're using applied follow-through faith. I went to work on my child before

I ever saw him, with prayer. And for the next four years, I spent at least four hours a day working with him, communicating with him through his subconscious mind, and up to 18 months old, we know positively that nothing happened, but that didn't destroy my faith. I knew something would happen. We kept working with him. We gave him every test available as to his hearing, and he wasn't hearing anything up to 18 months.

And then a strange thing happened. We knew he was hearing. We didn't know how much he was hearing, but when I snapped my fingers behind him, he turned to see where the noise came from. We knew he was hearing. By the time he was four years of age, we had developed 65 percent of his normal hearing through my prayers and my communications through his subconscious mind. Which of the two did the most good? I don't know. Maybe it was the combination of the two.

Sixty-five percent of his normal hearing was enough to get him through grade school, high school, and the third year of college. During that third year in college, the Acousticon Company, which makes hearing aids, heard about the unusual case, the only one of its kind in the world where a child born without ears ever learned to hear or to speak. Representatives came to the University of West Virginia at Morgantown and made our son a special hearing aid that gave him the other 35 percent of his normal hearing. Today he has 100 percent of his normal hearing—just like I said he would have.

Doctors came from around the world. Hundreds and hundreds of X-rays were made of his brain after it was determined that 65 percent of his normal hearing had been developed. They wanted to find any physical organ through which he was hearing; none was ever found. Another odd thing, Blair can hear just as well with his hearing aid on his spine, about as clear as he can with it on his head. Just as well.

I talked to Dr. Irving Voorhes, a distinguished ear specialist in New York who had the privilege of examining Blair. I asked Dr. Voorhees what he thought had happened that enabled this child to hear. "Well," he said, "undoubtedly, it was the process that you went through in dealing with him, whatever it was, undoubtedly that was what happened. And if you hadn't have done that, he undoubtedly would have been deaf, just like all other children who have been born under the same circumstances."

Blair today has 100 percent of his hearing. He's a successful and prosperous businessman. He's getting joy out of life. And from the very beginning, I taught him that the condition under which he was born was no affliction at all.

It was a great blessing, because people would observe the condition he was in and go out of their way to be nice to him. And that's exactly what happened. It was a great blessing not only in one way, but in many ways. It was a great blessing because it enabled me to learn about the power of prayer as I never would have learned from any other source.

THE POWER OF PRAYER

There are a lot of people who give lip service to prayer, but that's just about all. I gave more than lip service. I threw my heart and soul into our child, and I made up my mind if there was any God, I was going to get through to Him, and I was going to get a response—and I got through and I got the response. If you think that doesn't take courage, if you think that doesn't draw on your source of faith, it's because you have never experienced what I have experienced. I've often thought what a great blessing it was that God sent me a son without any ears to let me prove to myself that there is no such thing as impossibility—to know that prayer can do anything and everything.

While I was advertising manager of the La Salle Extension University, I happened to meet Reverend Frank W. Gunsaulus. Dr. Gunsaulus pastored a little church in the Stockyard section of Chicago. He had a little bit of a following, not very many, and I imagine he wasn't paid any more than enough to live on. But he had a multimillion dollar idea. He had long wanted to start a new type of school, a technical school, where students would study "book learning" half the day, and would go to the laboratory in an industrial plant and apply what they learned the other half.

When he made up his budget, he found that he had to have a million dollars to get his idea off of the ground to start. He didn't have a million dollars. He thought about this great idea for four or five years, procrastinated. And then he did something unusual. Without ever having heard of the Science of Personal Achievement or of Napoleon Hill, he commenced to use lesson number one—Definiteness of Purpose, or Primary Purpose. He got up one morning and said, "I'm going to raise a million dollars. I'm going to do it within one week, and I'm going to do it myself, alone."

He wrote a sermon entitled, "What I Would Do if I Had a Million Dollars," and announced in the *Chicago Tribune* that he would preach on that subject the next Sunday. He wrote out his speech word for word, rehearsed it, and went over it. And on the Sunday morning when he was to deliver the sermon, he went into his bathroom before he went to church, knelt down on the bathroom floor, and prayed for one hour that someone would see that announcement in the *Chicago Tribune* who had a million dollars and would hear his sermon and supply the million dollars for him.

When he was sure his prayer was received, he jumped up and ran. When he arrived at his church, two miles away, he reached into his pocket for his notes as he walked toward his pulpit. Lo and behold, the notes weren't there. He had left them on the bathroom floor. He said, "Well, Lord, it's up to you and me. I've done all I can do, and Lord, I hope that you'll help me out, because if I ever needed you, I need you now."

I talked to some of his parishioners years later, and they said that he stood behind that pulpit and delivered a sermon the likes of which they never heard before and never heard afterward. He told the audience what he would do if he had a million dollars, why he needed it, how it would change people's lives, and outlined his plan.

When he finished, a stranger who was sitting in the last row got up and walked slowly down the aisle. He reached up and took Dr. Gunsaulus's hand, pulled him over, and whispered for a few moments in his ear. Then the man walked back and sat down. Dr. Gunsaulus said, "My friends, you have just witnessed a miracle. The gentleman who just walked down the aisle and shook hands with me is Philip D. Armour, and he says that if I will come down to his office, he will arrange for me to have the million dollars."

And that's how Dr. Gunsaulus got the first million dollars to start the Armour Institute of Technology in Chicago, which in recent years has been consolidated with the University of Illinois.

A preacher, in one week, raised a million dollars—because he was definite about his primary purpose and took action. He believed in what he was doing. He knew it was right that he should have the million dollars, and he laid out a plan and moved on it.

The trouble with most of us is that when we lay out a plan, we sleep on it. We procrastinate over it. We dream about it, but we don't take action on it. That's not applied faith. If you don't do something that poses a risk in connection with your faith, it's not applied faith. It's just blanket faith. You have to follow through faith with action, and that's just what most people don't do.

MAKE UP YOUR MIND

I had an interesting experiment in the commercial field with my former manager, W. Clement Stone. Mr. Stone's estate adjoins the campus of Northwestern University, and he became acquainted with a number of the professors at Northwestern. One of the professors went to Stone's house one evening and said, "I've been at the Northwestern University quite a while. I'm just about making a living. I have some young children coming along, and I decided that I had to do something about making a greater income. So I went into the insurance business. I have a job now with an insurance company; I'm going to sell insurance, and I just wondered, knowing how successful you are in the insurance business, I wondered if you mind giving me the names of ten or fifteen people as prospects whom I may call on and use your name."

Mr. Stone said, "I'll be delighted to do that. If you come down to the office tomorrow morning, I'll have my secretary make them out and have them all neatly fixed on cards for you."

And when the man went down the next morning, Mr. Stone called him in and gave him the cards. The man said, "Now, Mr. Stone, is it all right for me to use your name?"

Mr. Stone said, "Exactly. Right. You can just tell them it was at my request that you're calling on them."

The man went to work with cards in hand, and before the end of the week, he ran back and said, "Mr. Stone, Mr. Stone, I've sold eight out of the ten, and I have appointments with the other two! Won't you please make me out ten more cards?"

Mr. Stone said, "Well, you hit me at a bad time. I'm busy right now, but here's the telephone book. You can copy them out of there. That's where I got the names."

And the man said, "No, you didn't."

Mr. Stone said, "Yes. I started with As. I got one out of the As, one out of the Bs, one out of the Cs, one out of the Ds, right on down to ten cards. And you can do the same thing. You can copy just as well as I can."

The man was shocked. He couldn't believe what Mr. Stone said, but Stone finally convinced him and then said, "Now you sit down and make up ten cards." And he did. The man made up ten cards and went out and worked a whole week—and didn't get an interview except on two occasions, let alone make a sale.

The fault was in the man's head.

What happened? Was it the prospects' fault he didn't get an interview and didn't make a sale? No, they had nothing to do with it. The fault was in the man's head. He didn't believe he could make a sale. He didn't believe he could take a name out of a telephone book and go out cold turkey, so to speak, get an interview and make a sale. He didn't believe that.

But when Mr. Stone gave him ten cards and he could say, "Mr. Stone sent me," he thought that had a great influence with the prospective buyer. It probably had no influence whatever, but the mental attitude in which the man doing the talking did have an influence on the prospective buyer.

BELIEVE IN (SELL) YOURSELF

I have trained more than 30,000 salespeople. And one of the most important things I taught every one of them, and what I hope to get across to you: *No one ever makes a sale to anybody of anything at any time without having first made the sale to themselves.* When you study any great leader, salesperson, lawyer, clergy, any great anybody who's business it is to influence people, you'll find out that the ones who do the best job are the ones who have totally sold themselves on what they do and say.

Reverend Billy Graham drew large crowds, held their attention, and did a better job than any thousand ordinary clergy because he had a better attitude about what he does. He knew what he did was right. The clergy who doesn't believe his sermon message very seldom makes any converts. The matter of belief really counts. Follow-through faith and the capacity to believe is the most mysterious, the most marvelous, and the most powerful in the universe.

Another interesting aspect I have noticed about great leaders is their great capacity to "hypnotize" themselves into believing that they can do whatever they want to do. Self-hypnosis—whether you're afraid of that term or not is beside the point. You're actually indulging in this act every minute of the day, whether you know it or not. We all are. The person who has risen to great heights is no better educated, no brighter, no more intelligent than the person who has not risen. The only difference between those who have risen above and those who remain stagnant is that one group has learned how to condition their minds to believe that whatever they want to do, they can and will do.

> **You can condition your mind to believe whatever you want to do, and you can do it.**

One day I was called in by the superintendent of the New York Life Insurance Company in the New York agency. I was told, "Mr. Hill, we have a salesman here who, up until a couple of years ago, led every man on the staff; now he's gone sour and is thinking about quitting. His sales have dropped to practically nothing. We want to know if you would analyze him and find what the trouble is."

"Well, yes, I'll be very glad to," I said.

They brought him in. His name was James C. Spring, and he was 65 years young. I talked to Mr. Spring for a little while and soon found out what happened. His wife made the mistake one day of referring to him as, "The old man." And suddenly he became an old man. Too old to sell.

"Mr. Spring, do you have some prospects?" I asked.

"Oh, yes, I have a pocket full of them," he said.

"All right. Tomorrow morning, we start. You pick out ten, and we will call on them tomorrow and in the next two days. I'll go along and listen. I won't say a word, I just want to hear your sales talk."

I could tell before we even approached the first prospect that he was afraid that the man was not going to buy. I could just feel it. His fear was exuding from him and penetrating my whole makeup; and sure enough, the man turned him down. The next one wouldn't even see him, and that went on all day and into the next. He didn't make a sale and didn't get but two interviews out of the ten. I knew then what had to be done.

Back at the agency, I told the supervisor, "I know what's wrong with Mr. Spring, and I'm going to tell him what the remedy is. He hears the word no before he even sees the man he's going to sell to. Before he goes in, he knows the man's going to say no. And by golly, generally he does, because the prospect picks up out of Spring's mind exactly what Spring's thinking. That happens in every case where two people come together as prospect and salesman."

"Now Mr. Spring," I said turning toward him, "I want you to go out and buy one of those old-fashioned air trumpets. I want one that's banged up, showing that you've been using it a long time. Not a new one."

He says, "What the heck do you want with that?"

"That's my business. You just go out and get it and do what I said, and then we're going to go over that same list of prospects we went over last week. And when someone says no, I want you to put that trumpet right up to your ear and make out like you didn't hear him, and go right on talking."

That's just what he did and you know what happened? Mr. Spring got back on track, and he excelled his previous record. For the next six years, he led everybody in the New York division of the New York Life Insurance Company. Isn't that astounding! It's amazing what a little psychology can do to change someone's mental attitude from fear to applied faith.

CONDITION YOUR MIND

You have to learn to work some tricks on yourself, too. The subconscious mind doesn't know the difference between a penny and a million dollars. It doesn't know the difference between success and failure, and will work just as hard to make a failure out of you as it will to make a success out of you. If you don't condition your mind by keeping your subconscious mind working with and for what you want and away from the things you don't want, you've lost the battle.

As mentioned previously, the majority of people spend the majority of their lives worrying and fearing and fretting over what they don't want, and that's exactly what they get out of life.

I try to make allowances for the weaknesses and the mistakes of other people who affect my interests. I don't always do a good job of it, but I try. I try to keep my mental attitude positive at all times, toward all people, about all subjects. This effort on my part has gone a long way toward placing me in a position where I have acquired in this life everything I need, everything I want, everything I desire.

You too can get everything you desire if you implement the power of follow-through faith. To develop your connection, set aside at least an hour a day to think deeply about your relationship with Infinite Intelligence. If you're a religious person, you can make this a time of prayer. You know now that faith is a state of mind realized only through a properly conditioned mind. This conditioning is accomplished by clearing it of all negative thoughts.

CREATE A FAITH MINDSET

After clearing your mind of negative thoughts, there are three easy steps to create the state of mind known as faith.

- One, express a definite desire for the achievement of a purpose and relate it to at least one of the nine basic motives.

- Two, create a definite and specific plan to achieve that desire.

- And three, start acting on that plan, putting every conscious effort behind it.

When you do this, your spiritual strength supports your desire and hands the problem over to Infinite Intelligence. If you relax reason, Infinite Intelligence will feed the answer to your subconscious, which will in turn transmit it to your conscious mind in the form of a hunch or intuition. When you follow the instructions gratefully, you'll have done your part.

One part of ourselves we can all work on is our habits. Next, we discuss ways you can apply this career success plan to developing habits that lead to living a successful life.

> **With faith, keep a positive mental attitude at all times toward all people and subjects.**

4

HORRENDOUSLY HELPFUL HABITS

There are no limitations to the mind except those that we acknowledge.

HABITS THAT GUARANTEE SUCCESS

Habit is one of the most powerful of human characteristics. Cicero declared, "Great is the force of habit; it teaches us to bear labor and not scorn injury and pain." But a Baptist missionary named George Dana Boardman encompassed the vitality and reach of this cosmic force in humans when he said, "Sow an act, and you reap a habit; sow a habit, and you reap a character; sow a character, and you reap a destiny."

There is one destiny-forming habit that the greatest achievers I have known all recommend. It is *the habit of rendering more and better service than one is paid to provide.* Do this and you will benefit in many more ways than you can imagine.

GOING THE EXTRA MILE

I call this habit "Going the Extra Mile." The rewards from giving more and better service will come to you in several different ways. In addition to compensation far exceeding the actual value of the service you render, you will:

- Gain greater strength of character.
- Find it easier to maintain a positive mental attitude at all times.
- Have a permanent market for your services.
- Experience the excitement of new and stronger convictions of courage and self-reliance.
- Enjoy new surges of the self-starting power of personal initiative.
- Experience an energizing influx of vital enthusiasm.

The following are some other benefits from the habit of rendering more and better service than you are paid to give. Going the extra mile:

- Turns the spotlight of favorable attention on you.
- Enables you to profit by contrast, since the majority of people have formed and applied the opposing negative habit of rendering as little service as they can get away with.
- Ensures permanency of employment. You will be the last to be removed from the payroll when business is poor and the first to be taken back after a layoff.

- Develops greater skill, efficiency, and also greater earning ability.

- Leads to promotion, because it indicates the ability for leadership. Moreover, the capacity to assume responsibility is the quality that brings the highest monetary returns.

These are but a few of the major advantages that can accrue for you and guarantee success, *if* you develop the positive habit of going the extra mile in everything you do.

If you provide no more service than you are paid for, it is obvious to your boss and even coworkers that you are not entitled to any more pay, and your chances of promotion will be minimal. If you develop the negative habit of doing as little as you can, like most others, you will not be any more valuable to your employer than the other employees.

Don't ever let anyone tell you that going the extra mile doesn't pay off. It will, invariably, if you watch your attitude. *The principle of doing more than you are paid for always pays off.* And it pays off in proportion to the intensity with which you apply the principle.

Now let me give you a little secret I have found to be particularly beneficial. Don't apply the principle because of a hope of reward or any promises for extra pay or promotion. Get into the *habit* of going the extra mile because of *the pleasure you get out of it* and because of *what it does to you*.

FROM REFUGEE TO HORATIO ALGER AWARD

When Carlos Arboleya of Miami told me his success story, I could hardly believe how a Cuban refugee from Fidel Castro's communism could achieve so much in so few years, until I learned of his philosophy of success. He said *he used a combination of going the extra mile and enthusiasm, with a strong basic philosophy of positive thinking.* He overcame obstacles that would have crushed many and became vice chairman of one of the biggest banks in Florida.

Arboleya was born in Cuba, the son of a poor watchmaker. When his father became ill, Carlos was sent to live with an aunt in Brooklyn. But a few years later, as Mary Granius tells of his background in *Success Unlimited* magazine, his father's failing health caused Carlos to return to Cuba and work to help support his parents. Carlos was 17 and found work as a part-time messenger boy at the First National City Bank of New York in Havana.

Working hard, coming in early and staying late without expectation of reward, Arboleya was noticed and given a full-time position in the collection department.

"The banking bug really bit me when I took a job nobody else wanted as assistant head of the collection department," says Arboleya. "That's when I developed a real pride in my work. From there, I was assigned to open a new branch of the bank. We worked until five every morning, but got that branch open in a week. I really began to love the challenges and the opportunities in banking."

Studying at night, Arboleya became a certified public accountant and was such a good baseball player he was offered a contract to catch for the Brooklyn Dodgers, but turned it down to remain in banking.

While studying law and accounting nights at Havana University, he went to the Trust Company of Cuba to reorganize its trust department. Two years later, after successfully completing that job, he took on a formidable task at the Banco Continental Cubano in Havana, which was on the brink of bankruptcy. He came in as chief auditor, soon reorganized the bank, and helped put together 62 branches. When he left, the bank had $375 million in deposits.

By then, in 1959, the revolutionary leader Fidel Castro came to power in Cuba, overthrowing the government and embracing communism for the people. Arboleya believed in democracy, not a communist dictatorship, for his country. His strong and vocal opposition to Castro and his regime jeopardized both his future and his family's safety. When the banks in Cuba were confiscated in 1960, he fled the country with his wife and two-year-old son.

They arrived in Miami with only $42 and their possessions in a few suitcases. But Arboleya, who then was 31, was confident he would find work and the family would start a new life in a free country. But despite his strong experience in banking, Arboleya could not find work in any Miami bank.

"I spoke English as well as Spanish," says Arboleya, "and was willing to wash dishes, scrub floors. I just wanted a job. If I gave my resume to a bank, it looked too good. If I didn't give it, I would have no experience. If I wanted to work at washing the floor, they didn't need floor washers. That was the biggest frustration I ever felt, and some of the worst moments in my life were when I had to come back at four or five in the afternoon and face my wife and tell her I hadn't found work."

Arboleya admits to nearly giving in to defeat at that point. "I was getting desperate. Five, six, seven days passed with no money. I asked my wife, Marta, 'What are we doing here? Let's go back to Cuba.' She turned to me, pointed to our son and said, 'That's why we came here. We're not going back.' So the one time in my life when I weakened, she gave me strength."

The next day, Arboleya put aside his ambition and pride and took a job in a shoe factory as an inventory clerk, paying only $45 a week. He threw himself into the job completely. "When the bell rang at 4 p.m., everybody else left," he says. "I would sneak into the factory to find out how the shoes were made. I tore them apart. I used to hear the foreman hollering, 'Who broke up this shoe?'"

Arboleya says he has always believed in giving an employer more than he is paying for. "There are people who will give fifty cents of effort on the dollar they are paid," Arboleya says. "I will always give $1.25 of effort on every dollar I am paid."

Again, through hard work and going the extra mile to show he had managerial stuff in him, Arboleya was soon promoted to bookkeeper, then office manager, and finally vice president and comptroller of the company. Then he was offered the opportunity to return to banking. He was offered a clerk's position at the Boulevard National Bank in Miami, one of the banks where he had earlier been turned down.

Arboleya passed away at age 91 after receiving numerous awards and accolades, including helping those who came to him for financial help. He kept a shoe in a glass case in his office at the Barnett Bank of South Florida where he was vice chairman and chairman of the executive committee. The shoe was from the shoe company where he got his start in the world of American business and finance.

"The reason I have this shoe is to remind me that I came out of nothing and that I can go back to nothing. That way, the position and the money I have today will never go to my head," Arboleya said.

While he worked for the shoe company, Arboleya never gave up hope that one day he would get back into banking.

In 1976 Arboleya received the Horatio Alger Award given each year to top men and women in their fields who typify the "rags to riches" American dream. The award is given to distinguished Americans who became successes while dedicated to the belief that our American way of achieving success provides equal opportunity to all regardless of origin, creed, or color, and that this American way is the highest type of human relationship conceived by the mind of man.

When I asked Carlos Arboleya what his success philosophy was, he had about the best answer I ever heard:

"When I was a boy back in Cuba, everyone said I was a dreamer," Arboleya recalls. "But I believe that you can make your dreams come true. If you work hard, have *enthusiasm* and *commitment*, if you have dedication to your work and set your goals high, you can achieve your dreams. But if you go home at 4:30 and watch TV, you sure as hell won't get anywhere.

"There is nothing one person can do that another cannot, if he or she sets themself to the task of doing it, and in doing so, does it with enthusiasm. Enthusiasm is the magic in man.

"You also must have the determination to succeed, confidence in yourself, faith and belief in God, pride of country and flag, love of family, and respect for friends. Those are the true ingredients of success. "

Though a busy man in the banking world, Arboleya still found time to be an active volunteer for the Red Cross, handicapped children, and other charities, and devoted as much time as possible to the Boy Scouts and other youth programs.

"The future of America," said Arboleya, "is in today's youth."

I hope Carlos Arboleya's example of achieving success in business by going the extra mile inspires you to do the same.

FORMULA FOR SUCCESS

Now I introduce you to an equation I designed to illustrate the success principle of going the extra mile. I call it the "Q + Q + MA = C" formula because these are the initial letters of the equation:

Quality of service provided

plus the

Quantity of service provided

plus your

Mental **A**ttitude

equals your

Compensation

By compensation, I mean all that comes into your life including: money, joy, happiness, harmony and respect in human relations, spiritual enlightenment, peace of mind, a positive mental attitude, the capacity for faith, the ability and desire to share blessings with others, an open mind to receive truth on all subjects, a sense of tolerance and fair play, and any other praiseworthy attitude or attribute you may seek.

There is a definite relationship between going the extra mile and other principles of this philosophy. All of the principles fit together and are the links in the chain of success.

THE LAW OF INCREASING RETURNS

The habit of rendering more and better service than you are paid for gives you the benefit of what I call the Law of Increasing Returns and insures you against the disadvantages of decreasing returns, thus eventually enabling you to receive more pay than you would receive otherwise.

Every business has either a potential or a real asset known as "goodwill." While this is an asset not generally listed in the inventory, no business can grow without it, or even exist for any great length of time.

People who habitually go the extra mile for others develop personal goodwill that ensures them opportunities and advantages in connection with the sale of their services. Such advantages are not available to the person who does not practice this positive habit. This "goodwill asset" is generally known as someone's *reputation for efficiency*. Without it, people can't market personal services to their best advantage.

Going the extra mile works to the benefit of the employer, too, just as it benefits an employee. It is one of the most important principles through which businesses grow to huge proportions and business people accumulate great fortunes.

The following are examples that show how four companies grew and prospered, becoming giants of American business by having both management and employees develop the habit of going the extra mile in providing customer service.

The Southland Corporation—7-Eleven

Headquartered in Dallas, Texas, the Southland Corporation began in 1927 when the owners of the company, then known as the Southland Ice Company, came up with the novel idea of selling a few food items, such as bread, milk, and eggs, at their ice docks as a convenience to their customers.

Joe C. Thompson became president of Southland in 1931. When he died thirty years later, there were almost 600 7-Eleven stores nationwide. Under the reins of Thompson's three sons, there were 3,500 in 1970. By 1980, there were 7,234 stores: 6,600 in 42 of the United States, and 634 in Japan. "In 2022, 7-Eleven had retail sales of $30.15 billion in the United States... There were a total of 12,645 7-Eleven convenience stores in operation throughout the United States."[1]

Over the years, instead of trying to compete with the increasing number of big supermarkets, 7-Eleven stores continued to operate under the assumption that a lot of people who need only one or two items are willing to pay slightly higher prices to avoid the hassle of long lines and restricted hours. Many 7-Eleven stores now remain open not only from 7 in the morning until 11 at night, but for 24 hours a day. Going the extra mile in being open early and late for customers made the difference.

In addition to providing needed service to its customers, 7-Eleven USA also raises millions for charities annually. Also, 7-Eleven offers discounted franchise fees to retired or separated qualified veterans of the US armed forces. In 2005, the American convenience store chain was acquired by the Japanese company Seven & I Holdings; and as of 2024, there were 84,500 stores in 19 countries.

Lowe's Home Improvement

From its humble beginnings as a small hardware store in North Wilkesboro, North Carolina, and a separate, unpretentious lumber yard in the neighboring town of Sparta, Lowe's has grown to become the second-largest hardware chain in the US and globally. In 2024, Lowe's operated 1,746 stores and employed 284,000 employees, with a net worth of $123 billion.

Lowe's online mission statement: "We believe genuine relationships with our customers are the key to their success and ours. Whether you're a do-it-yourself customer or a professional contractor, we listen closely to your needs and deliver solutions that meet—and exceed—your expectations."

Not only did Lowe's provide a pioneer service to the home-construction industry, it has one of the best profit-sharing plans in the United States. Lowe's also offers their employees flexible schedules, family care leave, and tuition-free education assistance. Lowe's is dedicated to the belief that if its employees are happy, then sales and profits will soar—and that's also why Lowe's keeps rapidly expanding. Giving more and better service to customers is the foundation on which Lowe's was built.

McDonald's

"Ray Kroc has been called the Henry Ford of the fast-food industry, and some management theorists believe he has pioneered our society's successor to the Industrial Revolution—the

Service Revolution," wrote Robert C. Anderson, former *Chicago Tribune* writer and editor. "If so, history will recall his innovative organizational skills long after the Big Mac has been forgotten and the Golden Arches have become museum pieces.

"In my opinion," concluded Anderson, "the mainsprings of his success could be given the acronym HOPE, which stands for Honesty, Organizational Skill, Positive Thinking, and Enthusiasm."

Ray Kroc (1902–1984) not only emphasized system and service in McDonald's fast-food operation, he also insisted on quality—both in advertising and in the purchasing and preparation of food. To achieve this end, he developed Hamburger University, where McDonald's franchisees—both owners and operators—are given a three-week course in the company's methods.

Students at HU are thoroughly drilled in Kroc's success principle based on QSC (Quality, Service, Cleanliness) and TLC (Tender Loving Care). To Kroc, TLC meant not only serving the best and most quickly prepared hamburgers and fries to his busy-but-hungry customers, but also providing them with clean restrooms (equipped with plenty of towels and toilet tissue) and a courteous staff generous with smiles and thank yous. Employees learn to always go the extra mile to serve and please customers.

McDonald's has grown into a multibillion-dollar success story ($193 billion net worth in 2024) and is a major contributor to philanthropic causes.

The Quill Corporation

"No company has a divine right to survive and to prosper. It is a right that must be earned year in and year out," is the "bill of rights" stated in the employee manual, in the catalog, and in the headquarters of the Quill Corporation in Lincolnshire, Illinois. Quill is the largest and most successful direct marketer of office products in the United States.

Quill was started in 1956 by Jack Miller with $2,000 that he borrowed from his father-in-law. In 1986 sales amounted to $180 million with a customer base of approximately 600,000 and 850 employees. During that same time, competitors appeared with discount prices. By the late 1980s, the Miller brothers, Jack, Harvey, and Arnold, didn't give up; rather, they strategically targeted better customer service and product delivery and expanded the variety and number of products.

In 1998, the three brothers decided to sell Quill Corporation, with sales of $600 million in 1997, to competitor Staples, Inc. for $685 million in stock.[2] Staples runs Quill as an operating division retaining the Quill name and logo. Quill Corporation's future was assured under the auspices of Staples that reported revenues of $8 billion in 2023.

These four companies could not have achieved the expansion and financial success they enjoy without employees and management going the extra mile giving more and better service than they are paid for.

THE OTHER SIDE OF THE COIN

In my book *Think and Grow Rich,* I describe my analysis of several thousand men and women who were classified as "failures" in their work life. I found it tragic that the overwhelming majority of people fail, as compared to the number who succeed.

The following are my analyses identifying 31 major reasons for failure. As you go over the list, check yourself by it point-by-point, to discover how many causes of failure stand between you and success:

1. *Unfavorable hereditary background:* Little can be done for people born with a deficiency in brain power. This is the only cause of failure that may not be easily corrected by the individual. However, the problem may be overcome through application of the Master Mind principle (detailed in Chapter 7) that provides problem-solving by collective thinking with others.

2. *Lack of a well-defined purpose in life:* There is no hope of success for the person who doesn't have a primary purpose or definite goal in life. About 98 percent out of the hundreds I analyzed had no such aim—most likely the major cause of their failure.

3. *Lack of ambition to aim above mediocrity:* There is no hope for the person who doesn't care about getting ahead in life and isn't willing to pay the price.

4. *Insufficient education:* Lack of education can be overcome with comparative ease. Experience has proven that the best-educated people are often those known as "self-made" or self-educated. An educated person has learned to get what they want in life without violating other people's rights. Education consists not so much of knowledge, but of wisdom effectively and persistently applied. People are paid not merely for what they know, but more particularly for what they do with what they know.

5. *Lack of self-discipline:* Discipline comes through self-control. This means controlling all negative qualities. Before you can control conditions, you must first control yourself. Self-mastery is the hardest job you will ever tackle; if you don't conquer self, you will be conquered by self. You may see at one and the same time both your best friend and greatest enemy by stepping in front of a mirror.

6. *Ill health:* No one can enjoy outstanding success without good health. Many of the causes of ill health are subject to mastery and control. These mainly are:

   a. Overeating junk food

   b. Wrong thought habits—expressing negatives

   c. Wrong use and overindulgence of sex

d. Lack of proper physical exercise

e. Inadequate supply of fresh air due to improper breathing

7. *Unfavorable environmental influences during childhood:* "Just as the twig is bent, the tree's inclined." Most people who have criminal tendencies are the result of an unhealthy environment and improper associates during childhood.

8. *Procrastination:* This is one of the most common causes of failure. Procrastination stands within the shadow of every human, waiting for an opportunity to spoil our chances of success. Most people go through life as failures because they are waiting for the "right time" to start doing something worthwhile. Don't wait! The time will never be "just right." Start where you stand, and work with whatever tools you have, and better tools will be found as you go along.

9. *Lack of persistence:* Most people are good "starters" but poor "finishers" of whatever they begin. Moreover, people are prone to give up at the first sign of defeat. There is no substitute for persistence, so those who make persistence their watchword will discover success. Failure can't cope with someone who is persistently moving forward toward a goal.

10. *Negative personality:* There is no hope of success for someone who repels people with a negative personality. Success comes through the application of power attained through the cooperative efforts of other people. A negative personality doesn't produce cooperation.

11. *Lack of controlled sexual urge:* Sex energy is the most powerful of all the stimuli that move people to action. Because it is the most powerful emotion, it must be controlled through alteration and converted to other channels.

12. *Uncontrolled desire for something for nothing:* The gambling instinct drives millions of people to failure. Profound evidence of this is the Wall Street crash of 1929, caused when millions of people tried to make money by gambling on stock margins. Gambling addiction takes a huge negative toll on finances, relationships, work performance, legal issues, mental health, family dynamics, and almost every aspect of life.

13. *Lack of a well-defined power of decision:* Those who *succeed* reach decisions promptly and change them, if at all, very slowly. Those who *fail* reach decisions, if at all, very slowly and change them frequently. Indecision and procrastination are twins. Where one is found, the other may usually be found also. Kill off this pair before they completely bind you to the failure treadmill.

14. *One or more of the six basic fears—fear of poverty, criticism, ill health, lost love, old age, and death:* These fears must be mastered before you can market your services effectively.

15. *Wrong selection of marriage mate:* This is the most common cause of failure. Unless this intimate relationship is harmonious, failure is likely to follow. Moreover, it will be a form of failure marked by misery and unhappiness, destroying all signs of ambition.

16. *Overcaution:* The person who takes no chances generally has to take whatever is left when others are through choosing. Over-caution is as bad as under-caution. Guard against both extremes. Life itself is filled with an element of chance.

17. *Wrong selection of business associates:* This is one of the most common causes of failure in business. In marketing personal services, use great care to select an employer who will be an inspiration and who is intelligent and successful. We emulate those with whom we associate most closely. Pick an employer worth emulating.

18. *Superstition and prejudice:* Superstition is a form of fear. It is also a sign of ignorance. People who succeed keep open minds and are afraid of nothing.

19. *Wrong vocation selection:* No one can succeed in a line of endeavor they don't like. The most essential step in marketing personal services is

selecting an occupation you can throw yourself into wholeheartedly.

20. *Lack of concentration:* The jack-of-all-trades seldom is good at any. Concentrate all your efforts on one definitive aim.

21. *A habit of indiscriminate spending:* Form the habit of systematic saving by putting aside a determined percentage of your income every paycheck. Having money in the bank gives you courage when bargaining for the sale of personal services—otherwise you must take what is offered.

22. *Lack of enthusiasm:* Without enthusiasm you can't be convincing. Moreover, enthusiasm is contagious and is welcome in almost any group of people.

23. *Intolerance:* The person with a closed mind seldom gets ahead. The most damaging forms of intolerance are connected with religious, racist, and political differences of opinions.

24. *Intemperance:* The most damaging forms of self-indulgence are connected with eating, alcohol, drugs, and sexual activities—and are most often fatal to success.

25. *Inability to cooperate with others:* More people lose their positions and their big opportunities in life because they are uncooperative. This fault causes more failures than all the others

combined. Being cooperative and easy to get along with is a quality everyone appreciates.

26. *Possession of power not acquired through self-effort.* (This includes children of wealthy parents and others who inherit money they didn't earn.) Power in the hands of those who didn't acquire it is often fatal to success. Quick riches are more dangerous than poverty.

27. *Intentional dishonesty:* There is no substitute for honesty. We may be temporarily dishonest by force of circumstances over which there is no control without permanent damage. But there is no hope for the person who is dishonest by choice. Sooner or later, the person will pay by loss of reputation, and perhaps even loss of liberty.

28. *Egotism and vanity:* These qualities serve as red lights to warn others to keep away. They are fatal to success.

29. *Guessing instead of thinking:* Most people are too indifferent or lazy to acquire facts that cause them to think accurately. They prefer to act on "opinions" created by guesswork or snap judgments.

30. *Lack of capital, financial resources:* This is a common cause of failure among those who start out in business for the first time without sufficient reserve of capital to absorb the shock of their mistakes, and to carry them over until they have established a solid reputation.

31. *Other:* Name any particular cause of failure you have suffered from that has not been included among the other causes listed.

This list should help identify your weaknesses so you can either alter or eliminate them entirely. You should know your strengths, using them to your advantage when selling your services. And you can know yourself only through accurate analysis.

Start today to establish horrendously helpful habits that will become commonplace and second nature to your personality, career moves, relationships, lifestyle, and fulfillment of your success plan.

NOTES

1. "7-Eleven retail sales in the United States from 2017 to 2022," *Statista;* https://www.statista.com/statistics/1130950/7-eleven-retail-sales-us/; accessed May 26, 2024.

2. Company-Histories.com; https://www.company-histories.com/Quill-Corporation-Company-History.html; accessed May 26, 2024.

5

INGENIOUS IMAGINATION

If you never see great riches in your imagination, you will never see them in your bank account.

There are two kinds of imagination: *synthetic* and *creative*. Synthetic imagination means combining or bringing together two or more known ideas, principles, concepts, or laws and giving them a new use. Creative imagination means discovering new ideas, plans, concepts, or principles. Creative imagination's source is outside the range of the five senses of perception.

We are mainly concerned here with the principle of synthetic imagination because it is the keystone to the arch of selling and becomes more alert through use! In this respect, it responds like any organ of the body or group of cells.

Ingenious imagination brings the highest price of any form of ability. It always has a market, and it has no value limitations. Business slumps merely increase the need and extend the demand for this faculty.

The most desirable and highest-paid positions are the ones imaginative people create for themselves. If you use your imagination, you can discover ways and means of stimulating business, even when business is stagnant. To solve a problem or fill a need, use your imagination! Your ingenious imagination can also lead you to acquiring the position and financial resources you desire.

There is always a need for new and better ways of doing business. This need is your opportunity to make a fortune. It is an established axiom of business success that if you find a need and fill it, you will become rich.

HENRY FORD'S GREAT IDEA

A hundred years ago when the first automobiles were being made, workers assembled each car atop sawhorses, using parts they either made themselves or were brought to them by stock runners who scoured the workshops of the area. It was a slow and costly process because it meant that autos were practically handmade and only the wealthy could afford to buy them.

Henry Ford studied the problem and came up with a solution adapted from a concept pioneered in 1793 by Eli Whitney, inventor of the "cotton gin," a machine that separated the fiber of cotton from the seed. Ford broke away from the inefficient method of hand-production in the auto business by employing a concept he called "work in motion" at his fledgling Ford Motor Company plant near Detroit in 1910. Instead of having a worker completely assembling the magnetos used on each Model T, employees would repeat one of two steps of the car's production over and over, while a moving conveyor belt carried the magnetos to the next worker. This was the start of the world's first factory assembly line.

By 1913, Ford's assembly line cut Model I production time from 14 hours to only 93 minutes. Today's assembly lines are more automated, many using electronic robots, but they all owe their existence to Ford's determination to solve a production problem. It made him a multimillionaire and enabled the average worker to buy a car, thus putting America on wheels.

MILLION-DOLLAR PROBLEM-SOLVERS

Henry Kloss was an audio buff who designed the first shelf-sized speakers because he knew many people, including apartment dwellers, didn't have space for larger speakers. His smaller speakers became the foundation of the hi-fi business in the 1950s.

In 1969, Kloss began experimenting with another problem, this one related to television. He wanted to find a way to build the first large-screen television set. His experiments led him to adapt the design for a four-square-foot video picture out of an old World War II system for radar display, calling his creation the "Video Beam." It soon revolutionized the home television industry as more people became eager to buy television sets with larger screens.

Kloss's Advent Corporation in Cambridge, Massachusetts, became a leader in large-screen television, and in the following 25 years, he founded three companies. He sold one to a major audio manufacturing company for $4 million—and annual profits from his other companies totaled more than $15 million.

LESSON FROM A RENT-A-TRUCK MILLIONAIRE

In 1935, James Ryder saw a need while working as a laborer loading trucks in Miami. Many people wanted to move either one object or a whole household, but didn't want to hire movers and a truck. So he bought a used Model-A Ford truck for $130, with only $30 as a downpayment, and started his one-man hauling operation. By 1946, he was grossing $1.5 million a year. In 1960, he received a Horatio Alger award and his stake in the company was worth $11 million. In 1978, Ryder retired and started other businesses with no success.

"He could have just retired with $20 million and a $100,000-a-year pension, but instead he lost all of his fortune," said Leigh Culley, Ryder's public relations rep for 30 years. "But he was not bitter one bit. He would say: 'I'm just another guy like you; I had it good, but it was just luck and hard work, and plenty of people make it and lose it. I had a good time and I'm happy about how life is going for me.'"[3]

When James Ryder died at age 83 in 1997, Ryder Systems chairman and CEO Anthony Burns said, "Jim Ryder was an entrepreneurial genius who knew how to dream. He was a man who cast a very long shadow, a man who, during his active years, made a dramatic difference in the business world."[4] Ryder Systems revenues as of February 2024 were more than $3 billion.

WHAT CAN YOU DO TO CREATE A JOB?

If you are already employed, take inventory of the shortcomings of the business and use your imagination to eliminate some of them. Or, if you are not employed, use your ingenious imagination to create a plan for improving part of some business you're familiar with, and you will soon find a place for yourself. Job descriptions can be made to order.

If you are employed and find yourself worrying about the possibility of losing your job, convert the time you have been wasting on worry to a better use. Create some plan that will improve your work or add to your employer's business. In this way, you make yourself a valuable employee.

WORTH THE RISK

A good example of someone who came up with an idea for improving his employer's product is Bill Gore. While working as a chemist for DuPont, the world's largest chemical company, Gore searched for practical uses for a polymer called polytetrafluoroethylene, today known as Teflon. After another DuPont team came up with a use for Teflon, Gore kept tinkering with the polymer.

In 1958, with the help of his son Bob, then a college chemistry student, Bill Gore invented a new product out of the polymer, Teflon-coated ribbon cable. Computers were then just starting to attract attention in this country, and Gore saw the potential for the use of the cable in the fledgling computer industry. He tried to persuade superiors at DuPont to manufacture his invention, but they declined, so he resigned and started his own company, W.L. Gore & Associates.

It was a big risk. Bill and his wife, Vieve, were both in their mid-forties with five children—two in college. They gave up Bill's salary as a senior research chemist to pursue a dream. He said, "In appraising the contributions I might make to society...I have no choice; I'm compelled to try to carry out my plan."

Other inventions followed the success of the computer cable, most notably Gore-Tex, the lightweight, breathable, waterproof fabric that has become a sportswear staple. "The company now employs more than 13,000 people spanning five continents and thousands of products across industries—from high-performance fabrics to implantable medical devices and products that reduce emissions, explore space and solve other complex challenges."[5] All employees own stock in the company and it is consistently recognized as a Great Place to Work.

"Bill and Vieve Gore believed in the natural, human capacity to solve problems in creative ways. They also believed that given the right work environment, people will achieve more than they otherwise dreamed possible."[6]

In 2020, *Forbes* listed the Gore family as one of "America's Richest Families" with a net worth of $8.2 billion and among the 200 largest privately held US companies.

WOMEN IN THE OUTDOORS

The northern Minnesota wilderness lake country is about as far as you can get away from the hum of computers in the offices of the nation, but that is where the need was for Susan Eckert. Though she had almost completed work for a master's degree in nutrition, a divorce led Susan to rethink her career and life.

While on a canoe trip with a friend, Susan realized how rejuvenated she felt when spending a week outdoors with just the sound of loons calling on the lakes. She wondered how many women take wilderness canoe trips or go hiking or camping or mountain-climbing, to experience the mental and physical benefits of spending time in nature.

After returning to her home in a Chicago suburb, Susan left her studies and started her own business, specifically aimed at women over 35 who have little or no experience taking outdoor vacations. Since its beginning as a canoe trip, her business has grown to include hiking trips in the Swiss Alps, gorilla viewing safaris in Africa, yachting and overland travel on the Greek Islands and Turkish Coast, horseback riding in Ireland, sailing New England's Maine coast, and rafting the Colorado River through the Grand Canyon.

Susan Eckert, founder of AdventureWomen, died in 2017 after 35 years of planning and leading more than 500 travel trips worldwide. She found a need and filled it, to her eternal joy and the happiness of hundreds of women she helped discover the outdoors and, thereby, themselves.

YOUR BRAIN

Your ingenious or creative imagination is the "receiving set" of the brain; it receives thoughts released by other people's brains. Your brain is the agent of communication between your conscious or reasoning mind and the four sources from which we receive thought stimuli.

When stimulated, or "stepped up" to a high rate of vibration, the mind becomes more receptive to the vibration of thought, which reaches it through the ether from outside sources. This "stepping up" process takes place through positive or negative emotions. Through emotions, the vibrations of thought may be increased.

Vibrations of an exceedingly high rate are the only vibrations picked up and carried from one brain to another. Thought is energy traveling at an exceedingly high rate of vibration. Thought, which has been modified or "stepped up" by any of the major emotions, vibrates at a much higher rate than ordinary thought—and this type of thought passes from one brain to another through the broadcasting machinery of the human brain.

As previously noted, the emotion of sex is at the top of the list of human emotions as far as intensity and driving force are concerned. The brain stimulated by the emotion of sex vibrates at a much more rapid rate than it does when that emotion is quiescent or absent.

So, the broadcasting principle is the factor through which you mix feeling or emotion with your thoughts and pass them on to your subconscious mind. The subconscious mind is the "sending station" of the brain where vibrations of thought are broadcast. The ingenious imagination is the "receiving set" where the vibrations of thought are picked up from the ether.

Along with the important factors of the subconscious mind and the faculty of the ingenious imagination—that constitute the sending and receiving sets of your mental broadcasting machinery—consider now the principle of subconscious stimulation, or auto-suggestion. Subconscious stimulation is the medium you can put into operation as your "broadcasting" station.

Through subconscious stimulation, or habit-forming auto-suggestion, desire can be converted into a monetary equivalent.

Operation of your mental broadcasting station is a comparatively simple procedure. There are two principles to bear in mind and to apply when you want to use your broadcasting station: 1) subconscious stimulation and 2) ingenious imagination. You can put these principles into action beginning with desire.

The greatest forces are intangible.

Throughout past ages, humans have depended too much on physical senses, which has limited our knowledge to physical things that we can see, touch, weigh, and measure.

We are now entering the most marvelous of all ages—an age that will teach us about the intangible forces of the world about us. Perhaps we will learn, as we pass through this age, that the "other self" is more powerful than the physical self we see when we look into a mirror.

Sometimes we speak lightly of the intangibles—what we can't perceive through any of our five senses—yet when we hear them, it should remind us that we are all controlled by unseen and intangible forces.

Humankind doesn't have the power to cope with or control the intangible force wrapped up in the rolling waves of the oceans. Humankind doesn't have the capacity to understand the intangible force of gravity that keeps this little earth suspended in midair and keeps us from falling from it, much less the power to control that force. Humans are entirely subservient to the intangible force that comes with a thunderstorm, and just as helpless in the presence of the intangible force of electricity—we really don't even know what electricity is, where it comes from, or what is its purpose!

This by any means is not the end of our ignorance in connection with things unseen and intangible. We don't understand the intangible force and intelligence wrapped up in the soil of the earth—the force that provides our every morsel of food we eat, every article of clothing we wear, every dollar we carry in our pockets. But with dependency on Infinite Intelligence, we can control our actions and reactions to every and anything life on earth presents to us.

MOTIVATION: THE DRIVING FORCE

People become harmonious, loyal, and cooperative in their efforts because of motive. Those who achieve outstanding success, whether as individuals or as leaders of business enterprises, understand how to imaginatively attract the qualities of harmony, loyalty, and cooperation through appropriate motives.

Everyone who works for a salary naturally wants more money and a better position, but not everyone understands that better positions and greater pay come as the result of motive—of being motivated to provide more. The greatest of all motives that result in desirable benefits is giving more and better service than they are expected to give.

BEGIN THE HABIT OF SUCCESS EARLY

Going the extra mile at work is a habit that should be developed early in life. It comes from being helpful and volunteering at home, at school, and in summer and part-time jobs. Young people who pitch in and help others—either for pay or a positive attitude of service to others—learn one of life's best lessons.

Whenever a natural disaster occurs, such as spring flooding, or when tornadoes strike, you read news stories or see television news segments showing people pitching in to help their stricken neighbors. It is one of the most exciting and positive things to watch or read about, how unselfishly some people put themselves out, laying sandbags to keep a swollen river from overflowing, or helping firefighters and police come to the aid of a family whose house was demolished. People of all ages give generously of their time and labor, while at the same time developing a habit of going the extra mile that most assuredly helps them become successful in their work life. Aspire to be this type of person.

Sometimes pitching in to help others may not be as dramatic as volunteering to be useful in times of floods or tornadoes. Sometimes it takes just as much courage to go the extra mile when life presents success, but at a price too high.

In 2024, the headline read, "Miss New York Teen USA Declines Miss Teen USA Title After 2023 Winner Suddenly Resigns." Miss New York Teen USA is 19-year-old Stephanie Skinner. "It was an extremely hard decision to make. I worked so hard and sacrificed so much for this goal to become Miss Teen USA and although this title was a dream of mine, I believe one thing I will never give up is my character. For me, integrity and empowerment has to come first."[7]

Skinner founded Hands of Hope in 2019. She writes on her website: "Hands of Hope strives to instill hope and self-confidence in today's generation. Hands of Hope specializes in interactive, hands-on programs targeted at ages K-12 bringing awareness to the importance of self-love. Our H.O.P.E program presents on education and awareness for domestic and relationship violence for teens (bringing help, opportunities, prevention, education). My main mission is to show our youth how and why to love themselves unconditionally and create spaces of acceptance for *everyone*. I have completed over 850 hours of community service serving organizations such as, Best Buddies, Special Olympics, Girl Scouts, Feed My Vets, Ronald McDonald House of Charities, Operation Christmas Child, Upstate Cerebral Palsy, Gigi's Playhouse, and so many more outstanding causes! I believe in the power of giving back and aim to encourage community engagement nationwide."[8]

Bravo!

YOUR GREATEST OPPORTUNITY MAY BE RIGHT WHERE YOU ARE

If your employer is a successful business person, he or she is probably also intelligent and has the ability to approximate your value to the business. Before you make demands for more pay, or seek opportunity elsewhere, be sure that you are worth more by having first practiced the positive habit of providing more and better service than your employer has expected or demanded of you. If you have followed this habit long enough for your employer to have observed that it's a habit, you are in a position to discuss a higher salary. If your employer is successful and intelligent, your request will receive serious consideration.

Before deciding to change employers, seriously consider your boss and the business. Decide whether or not you are offered a future commensurate with your ability. If your analysis shows that an adequate opportunity exists where you are, develop that opportunity. You already have your foot in the door. You have your employer's confidence. Capitalize on this opportunity by making yourself indispensable, and very soon the law of increasing returns will reward you.

Competent farmers understand and make use of the law of increasing returns. They put this law into operation when they:

1. Select soil that is appropriate for the crop they want to grow.

2. Prepare the soil by plowing and harrowing and perhaps fertilizing, so it will be favorable to the seed they plant.

3. Plant seeds that have been carefully selected for soundness, knowing that poor seeds won't yield a bountiful crop.

4. Give nature a chance to compensate them for their labor, through an appropriate period of time. They don't sow the seed one day and expect to reap a harvest the next day.

Having taken these four steps, all of which have been in advance of their reward, farmers know that they will profit by the law of increasing returns when harvest time arrives. They know they will get back from their labor not merely the amount of seed they planted in the soil, but a greatly increased quantity.

Marketing personal services effectively involves this same principle:

1. Carefully prepare the soil where you will plant the seed of service by selecting an employer who is intelligent and successful.

2. Cultivate the soil and prepare it through harmonious and cooperative conduct.

3. Plant in the soil the finest seed of service, and be sure to plant an abundance of seed, since not all seeds will germinate and grow.

4. Don't expect to harvest a crop of pay before you sow the seed of service. After the seed has been sown, don't become impatient if you don't reap your reward immediately. Give the seed time to germinate. Meanwhile, you are making yourself indispensable to your employer and ensuring permanent employment.

If after you have done your part your employer doesn't show appreciation, don't stop sowing the seed of service that is right in both quality and quantity. Keep sowing as it will provide you with evidence of your ability if you should find it necessary to seek employment elsewhere.

The habit of changing positions frequently places you at a disadvantage of diminishing returns, because no employer wants to permit a rolling stone to upset the stability of the business. Remember this before you decide to change employers.

TEN DEMANDMENTS

A factory manager once completed a list of suggestions, ten epigrammatic bits of advice that he passed along to his employees. The following are his Ten Demandments:

1. Don't lie. It wastes my time and yours. I am sure to catch you in the end, and that is the wrong end.

2. Watch your work, not the clock. A long day's work makes a long day short; and a short day's work makes thy face long.

3. Give me more than I expect, and I will give you more than you expect. I can afford to increase your pay if you increase my profits.

4. You owe so much to yourself that you cannot afford to owe anybody else. Keep out of debt, or keep out of my shops.

5. Dishonesty is never an accident. Good men, like good women, never see temptation when they meet it.

6. Mind your own business, and in time you'll have a business of your own to mind.

7. Don't do anything here which hurts your self-respect. An employee who is willing to steal *for* me is willing to steal *from* me.

8. It is none of my business what you do at night. But if dissipation affects what you do the next day,

and you do half as much as I demand, you'll last half as long as you hoped.

9. Don't tell me what I'd like to hear, but what I ought to hear. I don't want a valet to my vanity, but one for my money.

10. Don't kick if I kick. If you're worth correcting, you're worth keeping. I don't waste time cutting specks out of rotten apples.

Follow these ten rules of good stewardship and develop the positive habit of going the extra mile, rendering more and better service than you are paid to do, and you will soon reap the rewards of climbing the heights to success and building a fortune besides.

THE WAY TO CREATE YOUR OWN JOB

Whether you work within a company where you are employed or start your own business, the most exciting rewards in career satisfaction and financial success come to those who use their ingenious imagination and talent to create their own positions. How do you go about it? The following are some steps to take to accomplish what you now might think is impossible.

1. Become thoroughly familiar with the job you are hired to perform.

2. Do your very best at that position. Go the extra mile to give more and better service than you are hired to give.

3. Study the work of others doing the same work or those whose work is dependent in any way on yours and the complete success of the department or the company. Are you and they performing as successfully as possible?

4. Look for ways to improve your own efficiency or that of the department as a whole. Can existing work be done better, or is something or someone missing who is needed to improve the quality and/or efficiency and cost-effectiveness of the position or operation?

5. When you are sure you have a solution to the problem, perhaps after consulting with coworkers or supervisors in a master mind alliance (see Chapter 7), write a proposal detailing your suggestion. Offer it to management and be prepared to defend your suggestion to the fullest. If it is your intention and to your benefit that a new position be created that will increase quality, efficiency, and cost-effectiveness, suggest yourself for the position.

6. If more education or training is required, go the extra mile and acquire the knowledge or experience that will qualify you as the best person for the new position.

7. After you accept the position you desired and created, don't stop there. Work to fulfill the promise in the position you created, then work to excel in that position and, if possible, exceed your own expectations.

Use your imagination to create a plan that will improve your work or others' work, and add to your employer's business and profit. Or create your own job and your own business. *You* can become "the entrepreneur of the year." The achievement lies in activating your desire, primary purpose, faith, good habits, and your imagination.

TAKE ACTION

1. If you are now employed, consider how your work can be done better and more efficiently.

2. Apply the same criteria to the work of those around you, but avoid creating problems by doing so.

3. Is a new position the answer to getting the work done better? What would that position entail?

4. Are you qualified to take on that new position? If not, what additional information or experience must you acquire?

5. Master mind with coworkers or supervisors to solve the problem of how to get the work done better.

6. Determine whether you can be most successful filling the position you created at the company you work for or by starting your own business.

7. Can you think of other examples of people creating their own positions or businesses?

8. Has adversity affected your life? How can you overcome it and turn it into an advantage?

NOTES

3. David Cay Johnston, "James Ryder, 83; Found Fortune in Truck Leasing and Then Lost It," *The New York Times,* March 27, 1997; https://www.nytimes.com/1997/03/27/business/james-ryder-83 -found-fortune-in-truck-leasing-and-then-lost-it.html; accessed May 27, 2024.

4. "James Ryder, founder of truck leasing firm," *Tampa Bay Times,* March 26, 1997; https://www.tampabay.com/ archive/1997/03/26/james-ryder-founder-of-truck-leasing-firm/; accessed May 27, 2024.

5. "Our Story," *Gore* website; https://www.gore.com/about/the -gore-story#our-history; accessed May 27, 2024.

6. Ibid.

7. Anna Lazarus Caplan, *People,* May 13, 2024; https://people.com/ miss-new-york-teen-declines-miss-teen-usa-title-after-surprise -resignation-8646371; accessed May 27, 2024.

8. Hands of Hope; https://www.thestephanieskinner.com/hands-of -hope; accessed May 27, 2024.

6

PRECISE PLAN AND DETERMINED DECISIONS

> **Knowledge becomes power only when organized into definite plans of action and directed to a definite end.**

SEVENTEEN PRINCIPLES OF SUCCESS

In **Think and Grow Rich,** I reveal a set of principles for achieving success based on my personal interviews with some of the most successful American business people in history. Through my later association with my friend W. Clement Stone, who added his Positive Mental Attitude (PMA) philosophy to my success principles, a new formula for success was devised that I recommend to you.

If you follow these 17 principles, they can lead you to overcome *any* obstacle and achieve *any* ambition.

1. A Positive Mental Attitude

A positive mental attitude is the right attitude in any and every situation. It is a conscious effort to replace negative, self-defeating thoughts with positive, self-fulfilling thoughts. Rid your mind of all negative thoughts and doubts and replace them with positive thoughts and ideas—and you can absolutely achieve any goal you set for yourself.

2. Primary Purpose

Knowing your primary purpose is the starting point for all achievements. You must first know where you are going if you are to have any hope of arriving there. A definite purpose is more than goal-setting. It is your road map to achieving an overall career objective. Goals represent specific steps along the way. Every action you take should ultimately boil down to the question: Will this help me reach my overall objective or won't it? Having a primary purpose enables you to develop a burning desire to help you focus all your energies on reaching your goals. Your main objective will permeate your mind, both conscious and subconscious.

3. Going the Extra Mile

If you do more than you are paid to do, it is inevitable that you will eventually be paid more than you are. Don't follow the example of others who may have the attitude, "When they pay me what I'm worth, I'll give them what they pay for." No. Give your employer more than expected. Render more and better service than what you are paid, and you will receive both personal and financial rewards to climb the heights of success.

4. Accurate Thinking

Every person who achieves any form of enduring success above mediocrity must learn the art of thinking accurately. The accurate thinker separates fact from fiction, or hearsay evidence. He separates facts into two classes: important and unimportant. Accurate thinkers learn to use their own judgment and to be cautious, no matter who tries to influence them. Don't allow emotions, biases, prejudices, or misinformation to cloud your thinking. Seek knowledge and truth, but approach all the "facts" with healthy skepticism. Recognize and relate, assimilate and apply information learned in any field to the problem at hand.

5. Self-Discipline

Learn self-control. You have the power to think and to direct your thoughts in any direction you wish. You also have the power to control your emotions. No other single requirement for success is as important as self-discipline or self-control. It means taking possession of your own mind for positive thought and to develop a mastery of both your thought habits and your physical habits.

6. The Master Mind Alliance

This is the coordination of knowledge and effort, in a spirit of harmony, between two or more people to achieve your definite purpose. Today it is referred to as "networking" or "group-think," which is collaborating, sharing ideas, information, and contacts in a spirit of perfect harmony to work toward a common purpose.

7. Follow-Through Faith

Many of the great achievers attribute much of their success to their strong religious beliefs. Many say they know they would not have been able to achieve success without the strength they gained from their faith. Follow-through or applied faith is not a passive acceptance of our spiritual existence; it is an active, positive application of our faith in ourselves, others, and God. Applied faith means taking action. Whether or not you share others' religious beliefs, you must accept the success principle of follow-through faith. Repeat to your subconscious mind that you are confident you will achieve the success you seek, and it will put your faith into action. Faith gives power to thought. If you think you can, you can! In addition to faith in ourselves and others, religious faith can be an integral part of the success formula.

8. Pleasing Personality

Your personality is your greatest asset or liability. It embraces everything you control: mind, body, and soul. The first step toward achieving a pleasing personality is to develop a positive character. Honesty and integrity are critical attributes of a strong, positive character. Your personality is the sum total of your mental, spiritual, and physical traits that distinguish you from all others and is the medium by which you will negotiate your way through life. A pleasing personality attracts the friendly cooperation of others and helps you gain both material and spiritual success in life.

9. Personal Initiative

Personal initiative is the power that starts all action and assures completion of anything you begin. Personal initiative is the dynamo that pushes the faculty of the imagination into action. It is the process of translating your definite primary purpose into its physical or financial equivalent.

10. Enthusiasm

Controlled enthusiasm is a priceless asset. It concentrates the powers of your mind and gives it the wings of action. Enthusiasm begins with your desire and primary purpose. Develop enthusiasm by setting a goal, believing in yourself and your work, acting enthusiastically and concentrating on positive thoughts. Honest, sincere, contagious enthusiasm will follow, and success follows enthusiasm.

11. Controlled Attention

The principle of controlled attention or concentration is the keynote of success in business and industry. Concentration on your major purpose projects a clear picture of that purpose on the conscious mind and holds it there until it is taken over by the subconscious and acted on. That is controlled attention—the act of coordinating all the faculties of the mind and directing their combined power to a given end. The word "controlled" is the key to thought power.

12. Teamwork

A simple cooperative effort produces power, but teamwork based on complete harmony of purpose produces superpower. Unselfish teamwork, an attitude of friendly and enthusiastic cooperation, can be a great positive force for individual and cooperative effort.

13. Learning from Defeat

Every adversity carries with it the seed of an equivalent or greater opportunity for those who have a positive mental attitude and apply it. Through a positive mental attitude and definiteness of purpose, you can find ways to turn defeat or failure into a force for success. Failure and adversity have introduced many people to opportunities they would not have recognized under more favorable circumstances. Analyze the reasons for a failure and you can turn defeat into a success.

14. Creative Vision

Ingenious imagination is the workshop of the mind, where old ideas and established facts can be reassembled into new combinations and put to new uses. Every other success principle leads to imagination and makes use of it. You will never have a definite purpose in your career or life, never have self-confidence, and never develop initiative and leadership until you first create these qualities in your mind and see yourself possessing them. The more you use your imagination, the better it serves you.

15. Budgeting Time and Money

Truly successful people budget the income and outgo of their time as well as they budget their money. Organize your time properly, and you will have time for all your needs. Inefficiency is a great time-waster. Unbudgeted spending can be as detrimental. Budget wisely and remember, *it isn't what you earn as much as what you save that counts in the long run.*

16. Maintaining Sound Physical and Mental Health

A healthy body and mind give you the confidence that, coupled with a positive mental attitude, will energize you to achieve your loftiest goals.

17. Habit Control

We can control our destinies and our potential for personal and career success only to the extent to which we can control our habits. Good habits that lead to success can be learned and established. Bad habits can be broken and replaced by good ones, at will, by anyone. Develop positive work and life habits, and you create for yourself a success track leading to reading your goals. All your successes and failures are the result of habits you form. You can change your life and control your destiny through forming a habitual positive mental attitude.

These seventeen principles represent the combined wisdom of some of the most successful people of past and current generations who generously shared their knowledge so you, too, can be a success in work and life. Some principles are repeated or explained in more detail in subsequent chapters. Repetition is done for a good reason. If you repeat an idea often enough, it becomes part of your thinking and your being and enters your subconscious mind. There, your positive thoughts go to work for you to help you find the inspiration and energy to put your ambitions into action.

At the basis of action is a primary purpose. I believe that 98 out of every 100 people fail all through life because they don't follow the principle of working with a definite purpose.

All you need to achieve success are the first two of the 17 principles and any combination of two others, but the more the better, of course.

Do you have all 17 steps to success within you? Remember, all you need are the first two and any combination of two others. If you need to improve on some of the principles, consider what you might have to do to score higher, so you will be ready when opportunity comes.

> **Riches don't respond to wishes. Riches respond to definite plans, backed by definite desires, through constant persistence.**

Do you have a burning desire to work in a particular occupation? Do you have an overpowering ambition to accomplish something specific in your work and life?

Those who reached the top in their profession set their sights on a major goal early in life, then developed a plan to achieve that ambition. If you do not yet have a main aim in life, or have a general idea of a goal but are not yet specific about it, get started now.

DETERMINED DECISION MAKING

Mastering Procrastination

An analysis of over 25,000 men and women who had experienced failure disclosed the fact that *lack of decision* was near the top of the list of the 30 major causes of failure. This is no mere statement of a theory—it's a fact.

Procrastination is the opposite of decision and is a common enemy that must be conquered. You will have an opportunity to test your capacity to reach quick and definite decisions when you finish reading this book and are ready to put into action the principles described.

An analysis of several hundred people who had accumulated fortunes disclosed that each had the habit of reaching decisions promptly, and of changing these decisions slowly, if at all.

The majority of people who fail to accumulate money sufficient for their needs, are generally easily influenced by other people's opinions. They allow newspapers and gossiping neighbors to do their thinking for them. Opinions are the cheapest commodities on earth. If you are influenced by opinions when trying to decide, you will not succeed in any undertaking, much less earning the money you desire.

Listen to your own counsel when you put into practice the principles described here by reaching your own decisions and following them. Take no one into your confidence, except the members of your master mind group, and be very careful about who you select for this group. Choose only those who are in complete sync and harmony with your primary purpose.

> **If you are influenced by other people's opinions, you will have no desire of your own.**

Close friends and relatives, while not meaning to do so, often handicap us with opinions and sometimes ridicule, which is meant to be humorous. Countless men and women carry inferiority complexes throughout their lives because some well-meaning but ignorant person destroyed their confidence with their opinions or ridicule.

You have a brain and mind of your own—*use it* and reach your own decisions. If you need facts or information from other people to help you reach decisions—as you probably will in many instances—acquire the facts or secure the information you need quietly, without disclosing your reason.

Keep in mind that everyone with whom you associate is, like yourself, seeking the opportunity to accumulate money. If you talk about your plans too freely, you may be surprised that someone beats you to your goal by putting your plans into action ahead of you.

Faith and Courage

In your search for the secret of the method, don't look for a miracle, because you won't find it. You will find only the eternal laws of Nature. These laws are available to every person who has the *faith and courage* to use them. They may be used to bring freedom to a nation, or to accumulate riches. There is no charge except the time necessary to understand and use them.

Those who reach decisions promptly and definitely know what they want and generally get it. Leaders in every walk of life decide quickly and firmly. That is the major reason why they are leaders. The world has the habit of making room for those whose words and actions show that they know where they are going.

Indecision is a habit that usually begins in youth. The habit takes on permanency as young people go through grade school, high school, and even through college without having a definite purpose. The major weakness of all educational systems is that decision-making is neither taught nor encouraged.

The 56 men who signed the Declaration of Independence staked their lives on the decision they made to affix their signatures to that very important document. People who reach a definite decision—to procure a particular job and make life pay the price asked—do not stake their lives on that decision; they stake their economic freedom. Financial independence, riches, desirable business and professional positions are not within reach of the person who neglects or refuses to expect, plan for, and demand what they want.

Persistence and Desire

Persistence is an essential factor when making decisions to convert desire into its monetary equivalent. The basis of persistence is willpower. Willpower and desire, when properly combined, make an irresistible pair. Whoever accumulates great fortunes is generally known as cold-blooded and sometimes ruthless.

Often they are misunderstood. What they have is willpower that they mix with persistence and desire to ensure achieving their objectives.

The majority of people are ready to throw their aims and purposes overboard and give up at the first sign of opposition or misfortune. A few carry on despite all opposition until they attain their goal. Let that be you.

There may be no heroic connotation to the word "persistence," but the quality is to the character of the person what carbon is to steel. The building of a fortune, generally, involves the application of the entire 17 factors of this philosophy. These principles must be understood, and they must be applied with persistence by all who accumulate money.

Unless you are one of the two out of every hundred who already have a definite goal you are aiming toward and a definite plan to achieve it, you may read the factors and then continue with your daily routine, never complying with those instructions.

There is no substitute for persistence! It cannot be supplanted by any other quality. Remember this especially in the beginning when the going may seem difficult and slow. Only a few people know from experience the soundness of persistence. They are the ones who have not accepted defeat as being anything more than temporary. They are the ones whose desires are so persistently applied that defeat is finally changed into victory.

We who stand on the sidelines of life see the overwhelmingly large number who go down in defeat, never to rise again. And we see the few who take the punishment of defeat as an urge to greater effort. These, fortunately, never learn to accept life's reverse gear.

Persistence is a state of mind; therefore, it can be cultivated. Like all states of mind, persistence is based on definite causes, among them:

1. *Primary Purpose.* Knowing what you want is the most important step toward the development of persistence. A strong motive forces you to surmount many difficulties.

2. *Desire* is comparatively easy to acquire and to maintain persistence in pursuing the object of intense desire.

3. *Self-Reliance.* Belief in your ability to carry out a plan encourages you to follow the plan through with persistence. (Self-reliance can be developed through subconscious stimulation.)

4. *Precision Planning.* Organized plans encourage persistence, even though a plan may be weak and entirely impractical.

5. *Determined Decisions.* Knowing that your plans are sound, based on experience or observation, encourages persistence; "guessing" rather than "knowing" destroys persistence.

6. *Cooperation.* Sympathy, understanding, and harmonious cooperation with others tend to develop persistence.

7. *Willpower.* The habit of concentrating your thoughts on building plans to fulfill a definite purpose leads to persistence.

8. *Habit.* Persistence is the direct result of habit. The mind absorbs and becomes part of the daily experiences on which it feeds. Fear, the worst of all enemies, can be effectively cured by forced repetition of acts of courage. Everyone who has seen active service in military conflicts knows this.

Before leaving the subject of persistence, assess yourself to determine if you are lacking in this essential quality. Measure yourself courageously, point by point, and see how many of the eight factors of persistence you lack. The analysis may lead to discoveries that will give you a new outlook.

DECIDE AND DEVELOP

You can achieve everything you want in life—including a career that leads to wealth beyond your dreams. All you have to do is:

1. Decide on a goal.

2. Set your mind to achieve your goal (following my proven-successful principles).

3. Develop a positive primary plan, or master plan, to guarantee your desired success.

The proven-successful information in this book shows you how.

From my lifetime of work on the subject of success, I offer you specific details. The following five-point formula is a tool you can use to discover your *definite primary purpose* in life:

1. *Write down a clear, concise statement of what you want most out of life.* The only criterion for deciding your main aim—whether it be great wealth, achieving the highest position you can imagine, or any other goal—is that once you have achieved it, you must feel you deserve to be called a success.

2. *Break down the achievement into units of effort.* Set short-term goals or objectives and make plans that are in the realm of possibility and probability for achievement.

3. *Develop a plan to achieve your greatest goal.* The plan need not be long. In fact, the shorter it is, the more likely it will focus on major issues.

4. *Set a definite timetable to achieve your goal.* Remember, major goals are seldom reached in giant leaps. Your plan should include interim steps necessary to reach the top.

5. *Memorize your definite main aim and your plan.* Repeat them out loud several times a day—almost like a prayer—ending with an expression of thanks for having received what your plan calls for. This is a form of subconscious stimulation, or autosuggestion, that I describe more fully in Chapter 4. Stimulation conditions your subconscious to accept as reality the goals you have set in your conscious mind. Repeating your goals aloud reinforces the messages that become helpful habits.

It is important to describe precisely *what you intend to give* in return for the realization of your definite primary purpose. There is no such reality as getting something for nothing. Everything has a price tag. You must be willing to pay the price in full before you get the object of your desire.

Make your plan flexible so as to permit changes. As you develop the plan for achieving your purpose, you may have to change the plan several times.

Some suggest sharing your purpose with others, but I believe it is better to keep your specific goal in life and your plans for achieving it strictly to yourself. Do not talk about it or tell anyone about it except the members of your master mind alliance. Talking about your objectives and plans can dissipate your enthusiasm, especially if naysayers add their opinions.

YOUNG AND OLD ALIKE

You think you are lost and floundering? You think there is no hope or future for you? You think the odds are too great against you to even try? Think again!

I have known young people who gave up before they started, or who wanted to retire and sit in a rocking chair before they even began their work life. They got nowhere because they lacked a worthwhile goal, and they let negative thinking drag them down into a pit of inactivity and failure.

I also have known young people who set their goal early in life and developed a passionate plan for success. Many had to overcome great disabilities and disadvantages, yet they got to where they wanted to be because of positive thinking and following a primary plan that led them to success and great wealth.

Which would you rather be—a success or a failure? The choice is entirely up to you.

I have spent the better part of my life meeting with some of the most successful and wealthy men and women in the world, asking them to explain precisely how they became successful and rich.

I share their secrets of achievement with you to help you form a firm base on which you can build your future.

You may be preparing to enter the workforce; you may still be in college or high school; you may already have a job but be wondering if it is the right one for you; or perhaps you wonder whether you are progressing fast enough. Whichever situation applies to you, it is most important to know what you want to do with your work life and decide on a plan to achieve your goal.

Finding the right position or career is seldom easy. Having a strong ambition to become a doctor, lawyer, writer, teacher, or other occupations may sound like simple choices. But the fact is that within these fields and almost all others, you must decide in which branch of law or medicine to specialize. Writers must choose to become newspaper reporters, television writers, magazine, book, or movie screenplay writers. And those who decide on a teaching career must pick what subject they want to teach and whether they want to be elementary, high school, or college teachers. You are, indeed, living in a world of specialization—so you need a primary plan.

For those without specialized aspirations, the choice of a career can be even harder. Most young people don't solve this mystery before they begin college. Many others graduate from college without a definite career goal in mind. They may possess a degree in a subject they were interested in and can lead to a job, but they haven't yet considered the most important decision—what career path is right for them, what to do in their work life.

CHOOSING A VOCATION

Choosing a vocation is a very difficult matter for an inexperienced person. Had I chosen mine at the end of my high school training, I probably would have become a telegraph operator, since this was the work that most appealed to my imagination at that time.

Fortunately, a former schoolmate who had been away attending business college came home for the Christmas holidays and sold me on the idea of going back with him. This decision proved to be very important in my life. For one thing, the training in business prepared me to earn a living. Second, it brought me into intimate contact with some of the greatest business and industrial leaders the country has ever known. In the capacity of secretary to some of these leaders, I literally continued my schooling with the men I worked for, and this part of my schooling was the most valuable I ever received.

I am convinced that every young man and woman should take a business course and gain some firsthand experience in many lines of business before selecting a vocation. This gives you an opportunity to weigh and consider the possibilities available in various fields of business and to choose a vocation based on actual knowledge of the details of the work.

My business training not only gave me the opportunity to learn, it proved to be a veritable insurance policy against catastrophe on more than many occasions during my 25 years of research, when I found it necessary to stop that work and earn money. There was never a time when I couldn't market the knowledge I had gained in business school for more than enough to take care of my living expenses.

Because of my business training, I was privileged to work for Dr. Elmer R. Cates and Dr. Alexander Graham Bell, inventor of the long-distance telephone. From both I received knowledge of a priceless nature that I share with you. Through this training, too, I was fortunate to work for a lawyer from whom I gathered a knowledge of law and legal procedure that has been most helpful to me.

Training in business brought me the knowledge to get every promotion I received while working for a salary. To it, I also owe the selection of my life's work with Andrew Carnegie, Thomas Edison, Henry Ford, and most of the others who were so helpful to me in building my work and life philosophy.

Those names may sound historic to you, and you might wonder if the lessons I learned from such men can be applied to your struggle today to decide on a vocation and create a primary plan to reach the top in that chosen endeavor. Let me assure you that they can.

What I learned from those giants of American business and industry were enduring principles that are applicable to you today in your tremendously important search for direction in your work and life. The principles I developed through years of interviews and other research into career and life success have been shared with millions of men and women through my books, including *Think and Grow Rich* and my career guidance course, *Positive Mental Attitude (PMA) Science of Success.*

Now I am aiming this positive mental attitude wisdom directly at you. In this and the following chapters, I impart the wisdom of the former giants of business and industry, athletics, the arts, and government. I also give you many examples of how top achievers in business, industry, sports, the entertainment world, government, and other vocations have made this wisdom work for them to become totally fulfilled in their life's work and enabled them to become millionaires at the same time.

THE VALUE OF ACCEPTING DEFEAT

No one plans to fail. But a familiar saying goes, "Failing to plan is planning to fail." Therefore, I now call your attention to a principle I believe to be the most important factor in determining success or failure in any calling. It may be described as "the faith and persistence to accept defeat," as being nothing more than a learning experience.

> **Life is filled with obstacles to overcome. Only those with the stamina and the willingness to fight can win.**

It has been my privilege during my public career to know many men and women of great achievement. All of them had met with opposition and overcame each one with commitment and persistence.

When defeat comes, as it will, accept it as a hurdle that has been placed in your way for the purpose of training you to jump higher! You will gain strength and skill from each hurdle you conquer. Instead of hating people who oppose you, thank them for forcing you to develop the strategy and imagination you will need to master their obstruction.

This is a beautiful world, and life is stocked with an abundance of everything you need, including riches and happiness. You can achieve these things if you don't overindulge yourself or allow yourself to be suppressed by circumstances and things you don't like.

Accept both the bitter and the sweet of life's cup like a good sport, remembering that a well-rounded life requires some of each. Success without defeat would lead to autocracy and consequent boredom. Defeat without the counteracting effect of success would kill ambition. Be willing to accept your portion of each, but don't expect to succeed without temporary defeat, for it can't be done.

How fortunate you are to be just starting out toward choosing or enhancing your life's work and forming plans to become successful and rich in it! You live in an age when you have the privilege of choosing any position you desire as your lifework objective.

Determined decision-making is the first step you must take, whether you are in school now or have graduated and are facing the world for the first time, or have experience and wish to make a career change. This choice, this decision, is a responsibility you alone must make, no one else can satisfactorily make it for you.

MASTER MIND MANDATE

> **No individual has sufficient experience, education, native ability, and knowledge to ensure the accumulation of a great fortune—without the cooperation of other people.**

Andrew Carnegie made a discovery early in his quest for success that enabled him to become one of the greatest achievers in this nation's history. It was a powerful concept that he called the "Master Mind Alliance."

The term master mind means "the coordination of two or more minds, working in perfect harmony for a definite purpose."

Carnegie made his massive fortune in the American steel industry—yet he actually knew very little about the steel business. His genius was in the ability to find capable people and get them to work together in perfect harmony toward achieving a common goal. That talent made him the richest man in America at the time.

In his steel company, his master mind group was an alliance of about 20 of his top executives whose combined technical knowledge and experience formed a whole that far exceeded the sum of the input of its individual members. Working together, they enabled Carnegie to make and market steel successfully.

Carnegie told me that he could have made his fortune in the grocery business, the banking or railroad business, or in any business that provided useful service to a large number of people just as easily as he made it in the steel business. In any business he chose, he would surround himself with individuals whose knowledge and temperament were suited to achieving success.

All truly great achievers have made a master mind alliance a foundation of their success formula. No one has ever achieved outstanding success in any calling without applying the principle. This is because no one mind is complete by itself. All truly great minds have been reinforced through contact with other minds. Every mind needs association and contact with other minds to grow and expand.

I employ Carnegie's concept of the master mind in all of my success motivation philosophies and urge you to take full advantage of this extraordinarily powerful tool for success as well.

To introduce you to the dynamics of the master mind, let me say that all noteworthy achievement in life is predicated on power. *Power is acquired through organized and intelligently directed knowledge.* The Master Mind Principle makes available unlimited sources of knowledge, because through its application you can avail yourself of the knowledge possessed by others, as well as all the knowledge that has been accumulated and recorded in books.

PERSONAL AND ECONOMIC ALLIANCES

There are two general types of master mind alliances. One type is for social or personal reasons, consisting of one's relatives or friends, where no material gain is sought.

The other type is the occupational, business, or professional alliance, consisting of individuals who have a motive of a material or financial nature. This type of alliance, which we will focus on in this chapter, is an economic alliance designed to help you sell your personal services, your skill, your ability, or to help you succeed in business.

Let's focus on the economic type of master mind realizing that power is essential for successful achievement in every walk of life. Also, remember that power is organized and intelligently directed knowledge. These facts clearly indicate that power in great quantities can be accumulated only through coordinated efforts of a plurality of minds.

No one individual, functioning independently, can ever possess great power, no matter how intelligent or well-informed he or she may be. The reason is that power must be transmitted before it is effective. One individual is limited as to the amount of power he or she can transmit or apply.

MASTER MIND EXAMPLES

Though Andrew Carnegie gave it its name, he was not the first to use the master mind alliance, and it has been practiced with growing success in the years since he coined the phrase. In today's computer age, it might be called networking of the highest order.

In this country, the first great master mind alliance was made up of our nation's founders. From the alliance of the great minds of the thirteen original colonies comes American liberty and freedom. The alliance between the great minds of the first states of the Union created a greater variety of opportunities for the exercise of individual initiative than exists anywhere else in the world today. American "know-how" is still the greatest in the world—and don't let anyone tell you differently.

The master mind mandate evolved on a global scale during World War II. What would the world be like today if the allied nations had not formed a master mind alliance? The United States and its allies were fighting for the continuation of personal freedom, opposing another alliance determined to destroy personal freedom. For any alliance to endure, it must be based on justice and fairness for all it affects.

On an economic level, Henry Ford organized one of the most efficient master mind groups known in the entire field of distribution. This group consisted of his thousands of trained dealers who operated in practically every part of the world. Through the cooperative efforts of this dealer alliance, Ford could estimate, well in advance of the actual building of his cars, how many could be distributed. He knew where his market existed and the extent of that market, even before the raw materials for his cars had been assembled. Ford owed his stupendous success to his understanding and application of the master mind principle.

W. Clement Stone and I formed a master mind alliance in 1951 to develop, further market, and expand the principles of success in *Think and Grow Rich*. This partnership led to him becoming my general manager, adding his positive mental attitude philosophy to our science of success course, and further enabling him to achieve his magnificent obsession of doing good works without thought of reward or recognition.

MASTER MIND MANDATE BENEFITS

Now that I have introduced you to the master mind principle, let's take a look at its benefits in greater depth. The following are some of the most important aspects of the principle:

1. Through a friendly and mutually beneficial alliance with others who have the information you specifically need, you gain knowledge—and knowledge means power.

2. An alliance of two or more minds in a spirit of perfect harmony to achieve a common objective stimulates each mind to a higher degree of courage than is ordinary, and paves the way for the state of mind known as faith. By faith I mean a state of mind when a person clears his or her mind of all negative ideas and conditions it for the inflowing of Infinite Intelligence. This is how inspiration is received.

3. A master mind alliance stimulates each mind in the alliance to move with enthusiasm, personal initiative, and imagination.

4. The principle has the effect of connecting the subconscious sections of the minds of the allies, and gives each member full access also to spiritual powers of all the other members.

CURRENT EXAMPLES OF MASTER MIND ALLIANCES

There are many examples today of master mind alliances at work. Computer consortiums share research, American automobile manufacturers align with foreign companies to gain greater manufacturing and marketing strengths, multinational conglomerates form partnerships with smaller but high-technology companies, and accounting firms form strategic alliances with public relations and marketing firms. The types and purposes of master mind alliances are virtually limitless.

One of the many consortiums nationwide is the National Semiconductor Technology Center (NSTC). According to the Center's website:

> The National Semiconductor Technology Center (NSTC), is a public-private consortium dedicated to semiconductor research and development in the United States. The NSTC will convene the U.S. government, organizations across the semiconductor ecosystem—including academia and businesses of all kinds—to address the most challenging barriers to continued technological progress in the domestic semiconductor industry, including the need for a capable workforce. As a new purpose-built, non-profit entity, Natcast was created to operate the programs of the NSTC Consortium. The NSTC Consortium, Natcast, and the CHIPS R&D Office will work together as a team to create a best-in-class new research center for the nation, based on input from members of the

NSTC Consortium and to fulfill the vision of the CHIPS and Science Act.[9]

In each master mind alliance, or consortium, are experts in their specific fields who collaborate and discuss matters pertinent to the primary purpose. Working in harmony, the researchers share their knowledge and work for the benefit of all and toward the determined successful conclusion.

12 STEPS TO A SUCCESSFUL MASTER MIND ALLIANCE

W. Clement Stone offers the following advice for developing a successful master mind group:

1. Be sure your master mind alliance has a definite purpose and that each member of the team fully understands the group's objective. After a careful analysis of your purpose, list the items you need to fulfill the purpose.

2. Choose members for the alliance whose education, experience, and influence best suit them for achieving the group's goal or goals. Do not choose people merely because you know and like them. They may be fine for social projects, but for your economic master mind alliance, you want people who have a similar definite purpose. A major requirement for membership in the group is someone with money to invest. Members also

must have the ability, personality, and willingness to cooperate with you in the alliance.

3. Limit the size of the group to the number of people necessary to get the job done. As a general rule, the smaller the group, the more productive it will be.

4. Decide what appropriate benefit each member may receive in return for his or her cooperation in the alliance. Remember that the principle of going the extra mile is important for the success of the group; and if you are the leader, you should set an example for the others to follow.

5. Set a definite meeting time and place. Meetings should be held in a nonthreatening environment. Explore all ideas in a setting that encourages a harmonious relationship between your mind and the minds of the others in the group.

6. Establish specific responsibilities and action steps to be taken. Each member of the group should be assigned one of the responsibilities, to provide research, expertise, or other means of solving this part of the whole.

7. Tune in to each member of the group. Try to imagine how you would react in a given situation, if you were in his or her shoes.

8. Pay attention to body language. Often the expression on a person's face or body movement

can say far more about someone than what they say.

9. Be sensitive to what is not being said, as well as to what is being said. Sometimes what is left out can be more important than what is included.

10. Keep the group working harmoniously. The major strength of an alliance consists in the blending of the minds of all members. Jealousy, envy, friction, or lagging interest on the part of any member will bring defeat unless removed at once. Make sure each member is doing their part and the group is working collectively toward achieving the common goal.

11. Know when to move the group along. If one person monopolizes the conversation, sum up the discussion and move on to the next point.

12. When the goal of the alliance has been realized, terminate the alliance after members are satisfied that there are no loose ends.

The master mind mandate is the basis of every great fortune.

Successful achievement is the result of power, and power in great quantities can be accumulated only through application of a master mind alliance. I have repeated this statement many times for the sake of emphasis because it is so essential in mastery and achievement.

The first step to take toward a successful master mind alliance is to get on good terms with yourself. Do some master minding with your other self until you are thoroughly acquainted with each other. This is one alliance you can't do without.

IMPORTANCE OF TEAMWORK

In my Positive Mental Attitude Science of Success Course, I stress the tremendous importance of teamwork in the workplace. I point out that cooperation, like love and friendship, is something you get by giving.

There are many travelers on the road that leads to success in business and happiness in life. You will need their cooperation, and they will need yours.

Cooperation was a major contributing factor in the establishment and growth of the United States of America, and its unchallenged leadership in the world economy that developed a higher standard of living than ever known before. American democracy is a splendid example of power and riches attained through mutual *teamwork* by the people.

The United States consists of 50 states joined together in a mutual cooperative alliance based on a Constitution that was voted on and accepted by a majority of the people of all the states. America's source of riches, freedom, and power can be directly traced to that intangible something known as "spirit" in which men and women work together for the realization of a common end. When the spirit of teamwork is willing, voluntary, and free, it results in a very great and enduring power.

The American way of life is friendly teamwork. It is founded on a philosophy of freedom and opportunity for all who make contributions to its support, in proportion to each person's individual talents expressed through a friendly system of free enterprise.

The same principle of friendly, cooperative teamwork applies to success in business and your ability to sell yourself and your skills.

Throughout life, every great victory is supported by some kind of friendly teamwork. Sometimes the wearer of the crown of success owes his or her victory to the unselfish *teamwork* of a spouse, sometimes to an efficient secretary or business partner, or to a group of loyal associate workers who help carry out the plans. It is a mark of great wisdom when anyone displays skill in winning the friendly cooperation of associates.

Cooperating through *teamwork* is most effective when your efforts are given without thought for personal gain, but for the good of others you work with or who will come after you, or for the good of the enterprise or company.

Until you become inspired with this broader spirit of teamwork and recognize the oneness of all people and the fellowship of all humankind, you will not be in a position to benefit from the principle of cooperative effort. Greed and selfishness have no part in this spirit.

Some say American workers have lost this broader spirit of teamwork in the workplace, and that adopting this community of cooperation principle has been a major factor in the great success of Japan in the world marketplace in recent years. Japanese management is based on two important principles: one is the concept of "quality circles"; and two, the general principle of workers as members of a corporate family.

JAPANESE MANAGEMENT PRINCIPLES

Jon P. Alston, professor of sociology at Texas A&M University who specializes in the study of human resources, writes in *Personnel Journal,* a magazine for corporate personnel directors, that Japanese work relations are based on three general principles: the worker is intelligent; all workers form a family; and the group is more important than the individual.

While these principles work effectively for the Japanese, Alston cautions that some or all of them may not be appropriate when applied to American business and workers. The Japanese are selective when borrowing foreign knowledge, and we should be too. But we should consider which Japanese policies may, in fact, improve our productivity.

The first principle of Japanese management is that a worker intelligent enough to do the work is intelligent enough to improve his or her own productivity. The problem is to motivate the worker to want to give advice.

In Japan, the first step taken to improve productivity is to ask the worker how this might be achieved. Workers might be asked to help redesign a machine he or she operates, or make suggestions on how to improve productivity. In Japan, 13 suggestions per worker are submitted. In the United States, fewer than one suggestion per worker is offered.

The Japanese assume that most tasks can be performed more efficiently by the on-the-spot worker than by an outside expert. This first principle of Japanese management can be put into practice in two ways, says Alston: quality circles and the constant upgrading of job skills.

JAPANESE "QUALITY CIRCLES"

Japanese quality circles are made up of six or more workers and their supervisors. These groups meet monthly or more often to study how to increase productivity. Quality circle members are given lessons on productivity problem-solving and quality control, and each is taught how to seek out and solve low productivity situations. Some even visit customers and suppliers to further improve the quality of their products and materials.

Many Japanese workers also take evening courses and other educational programs to upgrade their occupational skills. They also may rotate their work duties periodically to decrease boredom and work dissatisfaction. And by knowing how to perform a number of different jobs in the company, the employee becomes a generalist and gains a better picture of the work being done, thereby being more qualified to offer a wider range of work improvement suggestions.

THE JAPANESE "FAMILY" MODEL

The second general principle of the Japanese managerial system is that all workers form a family. The Japanese start from the premise that all workers in all organizational levels form a cohesive social unit, says Alston. Workers are expected to use all their talents to help the company. They are to give the company a loyalty similar, or greater, to what they owe to their families. Such loyalty means that workers do whatever is needed for the company's benefit, even if this means working overtime or taking evening courses in order to become a more valuable member. Nor would a worker leave "his" company if a better opportunity developed elsewhere.

In return, the Japanese company accepts a new worker on a permanent basis and promises lifetime employment.

Alston says it is obvious that not all Japanese managerial principles can be adapted by Americans. Nor should they be. Many practices demand too much conformity. But he suggests that American business should expand suggestion and educational systems for employees. Workers should be offered more challenging positions, work rotation, and more responsibility.

Quality circles have been introduced successfully in America and have resulted in increased productivity. Suggestions to upgrade efficiency and vary skills also can be beneficial to both employer and employee. They might help reduce mid-career crisis and subsequent work dissatisfaction.

At the heart of increased productivity and high employee morale in Japanese workplaces is teamwork. Some of the best examples of American teamwork can be seen in the world of sports.

FLORENCE GRIFFITH JOYNER

Florence Griffith Joyner was America's track sensation in the 1988 Olympics in Seoul, South Korea. "Flo Jo" set world records in the 100- and 200-meter events and was awarded three gold medals and one silver. But she was also a great team player, running on the United States 4 by 100-meter relay team to win the gold and also anchored the US to a silver medal behind the Soviet Union's team in the 4 by 400 relay, even though she was not scheduled to enter that event. She became the most decorated female sprinter in US Olympic history.

It took hard work—often enduring 1,000 sit-ups a day and sometimes crying because practice sessions were so strenuous—but she got used to it. The seventh of eleven children in her family, she knew poverty and sacrifice. She recalls days when there was no food to eat, and others when she and her brothers and sisters ate only oatmeal for breakfast, lunch, and dinner. But there was always love in her family to sustain them.

Griffith Joyner set her life's goal early. At the age of seven she was running in potato-sack races in a park. High school and college track successes led to her Olympic victories and after endorsements and retiring, she signed contracts for various promotions totaling more than $4 million.

Self-confidence was her philosophy of success, saying: "When anyone tells me I can't do anything, I'm just not listening." After she won her Olympic medals, she reflected on what they meant to her. "I laid out all the medals and felt the silver was the special one," she said, "because of the team's trust in giving me the chance. That silver is gold to me." Joyner died in 1998 at the age of 38 after suffering an epileptic seizure.

TEAM BONDING

To encourage teamwork in employees, employers, and any group of colleagues, there are thousands of DIY online suggestions and hundreds of companies providing activities and experiences that focus on working together to develop a sense of mutual trust and bonding.

Examples of companies that grew as a result of someone seeing a need and providing a team-building service include:

Let's Roam Teambuilding provides "Corporate team building scavenger hunts to boost morale, increase productivity and build stronger teams on an epic scavenger hunt. Our scavenger hunts are tailored by our writers to provide a fun and engaging experience for groups of any size...tailored to fit the time and budget of the group." Offered activities include art walks, bar crawls, ghost tours, virtual escape rooms, and a murder mystery party.

Impact4Good's website says, "We partner with groups to give back to their community. Whether in-person or virtual, small office team to full company all-hands, across the US or abroad, we bring community service to you. After discussing your team's purpose, goals and event, we'll pinpoint the cause you wish to support. From there, we'll walk you through the range of programs and activities we offer." Causes focused on include disaster relief, military and veterans, environment, children, animals, and hunger. "We want to learn all about you. Our partnership begins with us listening carefully—who you are, who is coming together, why you're motivated to bring your team together, what are your goals and objectives, and more. We'll dive in to understand not only the big picture, but the key logistics too, because every detail matters in coming up with the right options."

Athletes in Action's four values are: "faith, oneness, growth, and fruitfulness. Our values are the way we go about achieving our objectives. They reflect what it means to be a good team player within our organization and the way we develop leaders. In 1966, our founder, Dave Hannah, launched an organization to help athletes use their platform to share the hope of Jesus with the world. Beginning with wrestling, and then adding basketball, baseball, soccer, track and field, and volleyball, Athletes in Action has been building total athletes through high-level competition, spiritual mentorship, and training for a lifetime of purpose and mission. Since initially launching as a traveling sports ministry, AIA has grown into a ministry with staff members on college campuses, in professional locker rooms, and in athletic organizations around the world."

AVVA offers "Amazing virtual and online experiences designed for team building, company celebrations and corporate events." Companies can choose from more than 200 experiences to "connect your remote team and clients." AVVA's mission is to "provide companies with the very best experiences for their corporate events. With hundreds of hand-picked options available, we're committed to being the number 1 platform for choice and quality. Founded in 2018, we're routed [*sic*] in the science that shared experiences build connections and promote happiness in people. Since 2020, we've become global leaders in virtual and hybrid experiences and are passionate about supporting companies looking to engage their remote teams and communities. We're proud to say 1,000+ companies across the world now trust us for their team socials, client events, Christmas parties and much more."

COOPERATION AND TEAMWORK GO HAND IN HAND

Being a cooperative employee and a willing team worker are two of the most important requisites for success in marketing yourself and reaping financial and self-satisfying rewards.

Your position is your opportunity to show what sort of ability you have. You will get out of it exactly what you put into it—no more and no less. A "big" position is just the sum total of numerous "little" positions well-filled. Cooperation is the key.

And as a vice president of a major Chicago advertising agency told me, "Competition *between* companies is fine. Competition *within* a company is a disaster for everyone." Agree.

Be cooperative with your bosses and coworkers, project a positive "individual atmosphere," and you will market yourself as a positive influence on all around you. Be a willing team member and you possess a fundamental principle of growth, power, and wealth.

TAKE ACTION

- What kind of "individual atmosphere" do you project?

- Can you recall instances when you projected a negative personality and your "individual atmosphere" was harmful to others?

- When was the last time you were part of a team, in a sport, in school, or at work? How well did you perform as a team worker? Could you have been more cooperative with others and been a better team worker? How?

- Could you work advantageously in a Japanese "quality circle"?

- Can you regard yourself as a member of a "family" at your place of work?

- Are there any Japanese managerial principles you can apply to your American workplace?

- How well have you accepted responsibility at school or work?

- What other people, in athletics or other fields of work, demonstrate good team-worker qualities?

TAP INTO SUCCESS

You can gain *knowledge* and *power* by using the master mind mandate. The following are steps you can take today to tap into these tremendous aids to success:

1. Start organizing your own master mind alliance by first deciding on a definite primary purpose as the alliance's focus.

2. Join together with just two or three others whom you know well, who have a similar major purpose.

3. Discuss your purpose but keep your alliance confidential.

4. Give each member of the alliance a chance to serve as the leader for a specific period of time. One of the duties is to enforce a time limit on speaking, and another is to encourage each member to speak freely.

5. Re-read the 12 steps to a successful master mind alliance and follow the suggestions to establish a beneficial alliance.

NOTE

9. "CHIPS for America and Natcast Release 2024 Roadmap for the National Semiconductor Technology Center," *National Institute of Standards and Technology,* May 2024; https://www.nist.gov/chips/research-development-programs/national-semiconductor-technology-center; accessed May 27, 2024.

SECTION TWO

PERSONALITY

PROBE

8

BUILDING A POSITIVE PERSONALITY

A major portion of our responsibility as thinking people, regardless of our calling, is developing the ability to negotiate our way through life with a minimum of friction between ourselves and other people. This ability is a must to enjoy life, build positive relationships, and market your personal services effectively.

By "negotiate," I don't mean the process of arbitration. I use the word in the sense of guiding your way through life, the way a captain negotiates a ship through channels toward the home port. How we deal with reefs and shoals, depths and shallows, and how we deal with people, obstacles, and opportunities in harmony with ourselves and others determines the success of our course.

Unless you have a positive personality, it is difficult to sell your personal services and keep them sold. It may, in fact, be impossible.

A positive or pleasing personality is the aggregate of all the agreeable, gratifying, and likable qualities of any one individual.

A positive personality is an asset none of us can do without, if we wish to attain success. Why is that? Because it is through one's positive personality that he or she motivates others to help him achieve the goals he desires, and no one can attain notable success without the help of others.

From birth until death, every person engages in some type of selling every day. And *selling* in the sense used here means *winning acceptance, approval, or adoption.*

Much goes into achieving a positive personality. One of the most important is a *positive mental attitude.*

POSITIVE MENTAL ATTITUDE

What is a positive mental attitude? It may be defined as a confident, constructive, sure, practical, and forward-moving disposition of the mind over against any given set of circumstances.

A positive mental attitude is the *right* mental attitude in any given situation and is most often comprised of the *plus* characteristics symbolized by such words as *faith, integrity, hope, optimism, courage, initiative, generosity, tolerance, tact, kindness, and good common sense.*

To understand the importance of a positive mental attitude in your life, consider that it affects the tone of your voice, the expression of your face, the posture of your body, every thought you think, and every word you speak. It determines the nature of every emotion you feel. Everyone and everything that comes within range of your personality is affected by your mental attitude.

It is well known that a person with a disagreeable mental attitude will disturb the mind of every person encountered. A disagreeable person does this with his or her state of mind alone, without speaking a word or making an unpleasant gesture of any kind. This person need only walk into a room where others are gathered and a good portion of those people will become uncomfortable merely by the individual's presence, even though a word is never spoken.

An equally dynamic situation develops when someone with a positive, harmonious mental attitude enters a room. This person creates a pleasant atmosphere that projects comfort, harmony, and progress. This is because every brain is both a broadcasting station and a receiving station that sends and receives vibrations of thought.

At one time or another, you probably have had the experience of meeting a stranger to whom you immediately took an intense like or dislike. Psychologists tell us that this is because of the *thought vibrations* we receive from this stranger. If the person's mental attitude and thought vibrations are in harmony with our own, we like the person. And if our mental attitude clashes, we don't like the person.

Every place of business, every home, every classroom, every workshop, and everywhere people meet regularly has its own separate and distinct personality or vibration tempo that harmonizes perfectly with the dominating mental attitude of those who congregate there. Some people are so sensitive to these vibrations that they can ascertain whether the family relationship is harmonious or marked by friction the moment they walk into a home. They can do the same thing when they enter a place of business.

If you desire to exert a positive, wholesome influence on those who surround you, and cause them to feel that you have a positive personality, it is necessary to maintain a *positive, wholesome mental attitude.* It is the most important factor in achieving a positive personality and will express itself in all the fine and noble characteristics that attract others to you and win you their favorable attention and cooperation.

BUILDING A *POSITIVE* PERSONALITY

Though a positive mental attitude is the most important factor in achieving a positive personality, there are others. A positive personality consists of blending the following qualities:

- Flexible mind
- Sincere purpose
- Prompt decisions
- Common courtesy
- Tactfulness
- Pleasing tone of voice
- Facial expression and the habit of smiling
- Tolerance
- Keen sense of humor
- Faith in Infinite Intelligence
- Keen sense of justice
- Effective speech
- Control of emotions

- Alert and active interest
- Versatility
- Temper Control
- Hope and Ambition
- Temperance
- Patience
- Humility of Heart
- Appropriate Dress
- Good Sportsmanship
- Proper handshake
- Personal magnetism
- Enthusiasm
- Sound body
- Stress management
- Positive Self-Image
- Positive Associations
- Cheerfulness

Let's look at each one of these qualities more closely.

Flexible Mind

Because a positive mental attitude will cause its possessor to have a charitable, interested, and generous frame of mind toward others, it follows that it will generate a *flexible mind.* If you are genuinely interested in another person and see the good in that person, you will understand that person's ideas and attitudes and have sympathy even if such ideas and attitudes differ from your own. Flexibility of mind is the ability to understand and sympathize and adapt to a harmonious operation with others' viewpoints and ways.

Andrew Carnegie said, "Flexibility of mind was the one quality which gained for Charles M. Schwab the reputation of being one of America's greatest salesmen. He could get down on the ground and play a game of marbles with a group of boys, making himself one of the lads for the moment; then get up, walk into his office and be ready to enter a meeting where he was called on to make decisions involving millions of dollars."

Life is one continuous series of experiences in salesmanship through which you sell yourself to every person you meet in social, professional, or occupational contacts. The person who lacks sufficient flexibility to harmonize his or her mental attitude with others will not have a pleasing personality.

Sincere Purpose

The second important factor in achieving a positive personality is a *sincere purpose*—for which there is no satisfactory substitute, because it reaches deeper into a human being than most qualities of personality. Being sincere means you are genuine, honest, pure, true.

Sincerity, or the lack of it, writes itself indelibly into every word we speak, into every act and deed, and is reflected in our thoughts so that even the novice at character analysis can recognize sincerity's presence or absence. Being insincere means we are dishonest, fake, phony, two-faced.

Sincerity is the attribute that gains the confidence of others. It is an essential requirement in all satisfactory relationships.

The lack of sincerity shows up in the expression on a person's face, in the nature and trend of conversations, in this choice of intimate associates, and in the type of service provided at work.

Be sincere, first of all, with yourself. Be sincere with your family, your daily associates in connection with your occupation. Be sincere with your friends and acquaintances, and with your country. And above all, be sincere with the Giver of all good gifts.

Your sincerity will pay off in ways too numerous to mention. But the greatest of these will be the feeling of self-reliance you will experience.

Prompt Decisions

Prompt decision-making is a very important quality in a positive personality, and a very prominent trait in all successful persons. Making prompt decisions is a habit acquired through *self-discipline* and develops as a result of a confident, constructive, sure, and progressive *positive mental attitude.* It is closely related, as you will readily perceive, to a *definite primary purpose,* the starting point of all achievement.

Common Courtesy

It has been said that *courtesy* is the cheapest, yet the most profitable, of all traits of a positive personality. This may be an exaggeration, but it is not an overstatement to say that courtesy is essential to pleasing your associates.

Common courtesy costs nothing from our wallet. All it costs is a positive mental attitude, a sincere purpose, consideration for the rights and feelings of others, and a willingness to share your blessings. Notice how all of these principles are interrelated, so that the development of one leads to the achievement of others.

Courtesy is the habit of respecting other people's rights and feelings under all circumstances; the habit of going out of your way to help a less fortunate person whenever possible; the habit of providing useful service without the expectation of direct reward; and last but not least, the habit of controlling selfishness, greed, envy, and hatred.

Courtesy is a reflection of the spirit of fellowship without which we would have no dependable friends. Often courtesy serves as an irresistible force with which to disarm enemies and antagonists.

Tactfulness

Tactfulness is so closely related to common courtesy that it can't be separated one from the other. Tactfulness consists of doing and saying the right thing at the right time. Where courtesy and good common sense are applied, tactfulness will inevitably follow.

Lack of this quality has cost many people their jobs, to say nothing of their greatest opportunities. *Tact has been defined as the ability to make a point without making an enemy.*

The following are some signs of a tactless person. *Avoid these signs* if you want to develop and maintain a positive personality:

- Gruff and irritable tones that indicate a negative attitude.
- Interrupting others who are talking.

- Speaking out of turn when silence is more appropriate.
- Overuse of the pronoun "I."
- Asking impertinent questions to impress others.
- Injecting intimately personal subjects into a conversation that may be embarrassing to others.
- Going where not invited.
- Self-praise, which reflects an inferiority complex.
- Flaunting the rules of polite society in matters of dress.
- Making personal calls at inconvenient hours without prior notice or permission.
- Volunteering opinions that have not been requested.
- Speaking disparagingly of others.
- Correcting subordinates and associates in front of others.
- Presuming friendship or acquaintanceship in asking favors without a right to request.
- Using profane and offensive language.
- Expressing dislikes too freely.
- Criticizing someone's political or religious beliefs.
- Gossiping.
- Minimizing someone's achievements instead of offering sincere congratulations.

The person who carefully checks his or her personality by this list of common errors in tactfulness may make discoveries of great benefit!

Pleasing Tone of Voice

We express our personality through the spoken word more often than in any other way, and our voice often indicates our true inner feelings more than the words we use. So for a positive personality ensure that your tone of voice is controlled, pleasing, and clear. An uncontrolled tone of voice can cause the listener to suspect insincerity. A tone of voice with the suggestion of irritability or impatience can completely undo all the good that a well-worded, courteously spoken sentence might have done, had it been spoken pleasantly.

Many speakers can bring people to tears merely by their tone of voice. Often listeners pay little attention to the actual words of a speaker but are moved, either favorably or otherwise, by the tone and feeling put into those words.

There are times when you may feel compelled to speak with agitation or irritability in your voice. Try your best to avoid saying anything until you can control your voice, and thereby your feelings, so you can speak in a more pleasing tone. You will accomplish nothing by sounding out of temper—but you can accomplish much by speaking when you and your voice are under better control and you express *courtesy* to others.

Facial Expression and the Habit of Smiling

Two traits of a positive personality that should always be closely associated are the habits of voice control and smiling when you speak. The combination of these two traits makes yourself pleasing to others even under stressful circumstances.

The nature of a person's character can be read in the expression on our face. Everyone, consciously or subconsciously, tries to discern what is going on in the minds of others by studying their facial expressions. A smile or a frown convey the mental attitude of its wearer with unerring accuracy.

Master salespeople practice the art examining facial expressions. They can detect, by careful observation of their prospective purchaser's face, the nature of the person's thoughts. Moreover, they learn to judge what is going on in the prospect's mind by the tone of the person's voice. Thus, the smile, tone of the voice, and the entire expression constitute open windows to see what is going on in the person's mind.

The intelligent person will take care that these windows disclose to his associates only what is pleasing and attractive to them. Remember these three openings to the mind, the "big three" of the traits of attractive personality: 1) smile, 2) facial expression, and 3) tone of voice. Cultivate them and keep them always under control.

Tolerance

Tolerance is the disposition to be patient and fair toward those whose opinions, practices, and beliefs differ from your own. In other words, tolerance is the maintenance of an open mind.

The tolerant person leaves his or her mind open to receive new and different facts and knowledge on all subjects. This does not necessarily mean that you will retain and adopt these new facts and knowledge, but you will examine and try to understand, then patiently and wisely reach a fair conclusion.

The intolerant person, on the other hand, has fixed opinions on almost everything. He usually expresses these opinions freely and emphatically, and most often with the inference that anyone who disagrees with him is wrong. This is a trait of personality that never adds to popularity. Most people resent open confrontation regarding their opinions.

Keep an open mind on all subjects so you can grow mentally and spiritually. Always show a wholesome respect for others. Never forget that humility of heart attracts more friends than all the wisdom of humankind.

Keen Sense of Humor

A well-developed sense of humor aids in becoming flexible. Humor relaxes people and attracts many friends.

A keen sense of humor keeps us from taking ourselves too seriously and can provide an escape from the routine of the daily grind. Humor can serve as a tonic for the maintenance of sound physical health.

Doctors are finally realizing how beneficial laughter can be to our good mental health. Laughter can be a form of both physical and mental fitness. It can see you through a "down" period in your day and help relieve stress or disappointment.

Dr. William F. Fry, Stanford University psychiatrist, says humor helps us keep perspective, offers new points of view, and unlocks tension, "A good laugh gives the heart muscles a good workout, improves circulation, fills the lungs with oxygen-rich air, and counteracts fear, anger, and depression—all negative emotions linked to physical and mental illness."

Workshops are even offered for bankers, managers, engineers, and business tycoons, to help them use humor as a management tool. Maintain a good sense of humor, but don't confuse this quality with becoming the office clown or joke-teller.

Humor has its own special brand of chemistry, which when properly mixed with sincerity, courtesy, tact, and tolerance will develop a most positive personality and will have a definite influence in achieving popularity.

Faith in Infinite Intelligence

It is inevitable that the subject of *faith* must be woven into every principle of the philosophy of individual achievement, for the intangible power of faith is the essence of every great achievement. No philosophy of individual achievement would be complete without a definite recognition of the power of faith.

Faith in Infinite Intelligence inspires faith in human beings as well. If you have faith in Infinite Intelligence, faith in yourself, and faith in other people—they will be inspired to have faith in you. People of faith will cheerfully give their cooperation, so you can achieve your objectives and desires and successfully reach your ultimate goal.

Keen Sense of Justice

A keen sense of justice not only aids in the development of a positive personality, but becomes a priceless asset in almost every human relationship. It banishes avarice, greed, envy, hatred, and selfishness, and gives the individual a much better understanding of his rights, privileges, and responsibilities.

By justice, I refer to *intentional honesty,* the result of a constructive, wholesome, positive mental attitude. The justice

I speak of here cannot be altered for the sake of expediency, nor can it be stretched to fit any circumstance or to extend an individual's personal interest. The justice I refer to will motivate the individual to do what is right because it is right—not for any immediate advantage or hope of reward.

The rewards of a keen sense of justice are many and varied. The following are some of the most important rewards; a keen sense of justice:

- Establishes a sound basis for confidence.

- Develops a sound and dependable character, the greatest of all the attracting forces of a positive personality.

- Not only attracts people, but also offers opportunities for personal gain in connection with your occupation.

- Provides a person with a feeling of self-reliance and self-respect.

- Gives you a clear conscience.

- Prepares the mind for faith.

- Inspires you to move toward your definite primary purpose with greater personal initiative.

The justice I speak of here refers to *moral justice,* not *legal justice.* Moral justice is what someone voluntarily observes because of self-respect and a sense of responsibility toward others.

Effective Speech

For a positive personality, it is essential to choose the right words to say or write—words that will attract and not repel.

There is no excuse for the careless use of words that offend people's sensibilities. The appropriate use of words is regarded as a sign of education and culture, as well as character. The person who uses the proper words at the proper time has developed a very important factor in achieving a positive personality.

The appropriate use of words, together with a pleasing and motivating tone of voice and a pleasant facial expression, will go a long way toward gaining attention, respect, confidence, and acceptance. The use of profanity, at any time or under any circumstances, is wholly inexcusable.

The history of humankind reveals the trend of civilization being influenced by those who could dramatize an idea through spoken words. We have only to look into our own country's history to see the proof of this from the speeches of George Washington, Abraham Lincoln, and John F. Kennedy.

To speak effectively, combine several of the factors of a pleasing personality—appropriate use of words, a pleasing and motivating tone of voice or delivery, and a pleasant and dynamic facial expression.

The person who can't stand on their feet and speak with force and conviction, without fear or embarrassment, on any subject, is under a great disadvantage as personality is concerned. The same can be said of people who aren't effective in ordinary conversation.

In addition to the other factors mentioned in effective speech is the thorough knowledge of the subject. The greatest of all rules of public speaking is to *know what you want to say, say it with all the emotional feeling at your command, and then sit down.*

Control of Emotions

Most people are ruled by their emotions. And in the end, we all do what we want to do, whether it is reasonable or not. The following are lists of the most important positive and negative emotions:

Positive Emotions

- Love, a reflection of the spiritual qualities
- Sex, the creative force
- Faith, the source of humanity's greatest power
- Hope and desire, the inspirations of all achievements
- Loyalty, the foundation of sound character
- Sympathy, the foundation of the spirit of fellowship
- Optimism, the foundation of a positive mental attitude

Negative Emotions

- Fear (of poverty, ill health, criticism, loss of love or liberty, old age, and/or death)
- Hatred, the harbinger of friction among humans
- Anger, the beginning of hatred

- Envy, an indicator of fear
- Greed, a builder of selfishness
- Jealousy, a mild but very destructive form of insanity
- Revenge, a hold-over from the caveman age
- Irritability, an indication of unsound physical health
- Superstition, a mild form of fear based on ignorance

Each of these emotions, or feelings, positive or negative, must be brought under control if you are to achieve a positive personality. Emotion under control is one of the greatest powers known. Control can be exercised with reason and self-discipline.

Alert and Active Interest

For others to be interested in us, we must exhibit an alert and active interest in them. Indifference toward other people and their interests does not make a person popular or contribute to a positive personality.

There is no greater compliment you can pay someone than to concentrate your attention on their personal interests. And there is no greater accomplishment than being an alert listener when someone is speaking.

Alertness of interest begins with the ability to take a keen interest in your own *major purpose* in life. Without the ability to fix your interest at will on any desired subject through your definiteness of purpose, you will not recognize opportunity when it comes your way. An alert mind will see and grasp opportunity whenever and wherever it presents itself.

> **The alert mind usually gets what it seeks—indifference forces you to accept whatever life offers.**

Versatility

Versatility of interest in people and things is necessary for an attractive, positive personality.

The person who is only familiar with one subject—the one that most interests him—and knows little of anything other than his own job and affairs will never become pleasing to others. The more popular types of people are versatile. They have at least a surface knowledge of many subjects, are interested in other people and their ideas, and go out of their way to express that interest to inspire appropriate reaction to their own benefit.

Versatility leads to the capacity to understand people. It connotes an alert, thinking mind that continues its growth throughout life.

Temper Control

Losing your *temper* is the emotion of anger allowed free rein. Those who let their temper fly in all directions are sure to find it landing where it will do great injury on the rebound.

An uncontrolled temper and tongue have no part in a positive, pleasing personality. These people repel rather than attract, and most people stay as far away as possible from someone with an uncontrolled, sharp tongue. At best, most people talk too much and say too little. But the person with an ill temper often talks when they don't intend to and says many harmful things that are deeply regretted.

Control your tongue and your temper or risk destroying your chances of being liked and or accepted by other people.

Hope and Ambition

Hope and ambition give a person life and fire and inspire people to go on when facing defeat and hardship. This undaunted perseverance is a character trait others find attractive and worthy of emulating. People seek out the company of those who have hope and ambition thinking that perhaps a spark of their fire will inspire them to strive toward their goals with steadfast hope and ambition too.

Temperance

Temperance is the practice of moderation and self-restraint in all things, and is absolutely imperative in the development of a positive personality.

The individual who lacks the necessary self-discipline to manage his or her personal habits is never attractive to others. This is especially true of the habits of eating, drinking, and sexual relationships. Excesses in relation to any of these destroy personal magnetism and make the offender an object of contempt.

Moderation in consuming food and alcoholic beverages and refraining from smoking or taking controlled substances are virtues that have great rewards. People who control their intimately personal habits will most likely be a success in everything they undertake. There is no better teacher than achieving temperance through willpower.

Patience

We live in an ever-faster-moving, high-speed world, and the tempo of human thoughts and deeds is so rapid that we often get in each other's way. Patience is necessary to avoid the destructive effects of friction in human relationships.

Patience may be defined as calm and uncomplaining endurance under pain or provocation, and a quiet perseverance. On the other hand, impatience is a visible sign of lack of self-discipline that exhibits in a grouchy, irritable, disagreeable mental attitude. It rarely inspires sympathy from anyone.

A person who maintains a calm, confident, constructive, and wholesome mental attitude will find it easy to develop patience. That person can ensure their endurance by controlling personal habits, getting sufficient rest, and mixing work and relaxation in proper proportion.

Humility of Heart

Humility of heart is an outstanding trait of someone with a truly positive personality. Humility of heart assures the absence of arrogance, greed, vanity, and egotism. Humility of heart is the outgrowth of humankind's relationship with the Creator and the fact that all material blessings of life are gifts from the Creator for the common good of all humankind.

The person who is on good terms with their own conscience and in harmony with the Creator is always humble, no matter how great the wealth acquired or how outstanding the personal achievements.

When I think of humility of heart, I think of actor Harrison Ford. A friend of mine living in Hawaii with his wife and pets told me that Ford—whose acting career spans decades and earns millions of dollars per picture—and his wife and infant son visit them several times a year.

Why would a rich and famous actor spend days visiting my friend who works as an odd-job carpenter? Harrison and my friend were both odd-job carpenters in Los Angeles some years ago, barely making a living. Now that he is rich and a famous movie star, Harrison Ford has not forgotten that old friends can still be best friends. Ford's humility of heart preserves what he and his friend treasure highly—their friendship.

Appropriate Dress

Your clothing goes a long way toward giving a favorable introduction. Avoid overdressing or underdressing, and always strive to dress appropriately for the occasion, whether at work or leisure. The best-dressed person is someone whose clothes and accessories are so well-chosen, the entire ensemble so well-harmonized that there is no undue attention. Wearing proper attire in given circumstances gives a feeling of self-reliance and helps overcome self-consciousness.

Good Sportsmanship

Anyone who can win without boasting and lose without complaining is sure to be popular. This person is known as good, clean, and honorable. Colleges advocate good sportsmanship in athletics because educators know that this positive habit, learned in sports, becomes part of the athlete's character and is of great benefit in all other activities and relationships of life.

Poor sportsmanship is usually the result of greed, fear, selfishness, or out-and-out dishonesty. Good sportsmanship is an important quality in a pleasing personality because it inspires the friendly cooperation of others and connotes sound character.

Proper Handshake

Many people might never think of the habit of shaking hands as having anything to do with a positive personality, but it has, in fact, a great deal to do with this subject.

Most people when being introduced to others go through the ceremony of handshaking in a perfunctory way, not recognizing that indifference or carelessness in this respect may be as damaging as they are in other relationships. Some squeeze another person's hand until they cause actual pain, while others are so indifferent that they merely extend a hand that resembles a dead fish.

A proper handshake conveys animation, enthusiasm, and a spirit of sincere fellowship. It is done by coordinating a handshake with a person's words of greeting, generally emphasizing certain words with a firm grip of the other person's hand (not a vice-like squeeze), and the person's hand is not released until the greeter finishes his spoken greeting.

Personal Magnetism

By personal magnetism, I mean the sexual emotion. You may be surprised to find a reference to the subject of sex in a study of career success planning, but let me assure you it plays an important part in achieving a positive personality.

Sex emotion is the power behind all creative vision. It not only perpetuates life, it inspires the use of the imagination, enthusiasm, and personal initiative. There has never been a great leader in any field who was not motivated, in part, by the creative powers of sex emotion.

Don't be concerned if you have been blessed with a great abundance of sexual energy. But do be concerned if you fail to give this emotion its proper place as an important trait of personality by learning how to transform or convert it into whatever constructive or creative endeavor you wish to pursue.

Enthusiasm

People who lack enthusiasm cannot arouse enthusiasm in others. Enthusiasm is an essential factor in all forms of salesmanship, including the sale of personal services. Enthusiasm was one of the main ingredients in the success formula of S.S. Kresge, founder of the retail store chain that made him more than $200 million. When he was asked what his secret of success was, he replied that he went to bed early, arose early, worked hard, helped people, tended to his own business, was always enthusiastic, and always kept God in mind. He gave away most of his fortune to help others and leave the world a better place than he found it.

You too can ride enthusiasm to the top of the success ladder in life. Keep an upbeat nature and a positive mental attitude and visualize yourself achieving the goal you set, and it is yours.

Sound Body

You can't be enthusiastic if you're not in good health. Feeling good and looking good can be as important to your business and career success as getting the proper education and maintaining a positive attitude. Good health will help you achieve higher levels of productivity, enable your mind power to function at maximum peak performance, and give you the energy and clear-headedness you need to carry out your goals.

Start early to get into the habit of eating right, getting enough sleep, and exercising.

Nutritionists today tell us to stop smoking; include fiber in our diet through eating whole grain breads, raw fruits, and nuts; cut down on fats; eat citrus fruits and green leafy vegetables high in vitamins C and E; and eat foods rich in beta carotene such as carrots, dark green leafy vegetables such as spinach and broccoli, and fruits including peaches, apricots, cantaloupe, and other melons.

Develop good sleeping habits by arranging your schedule so you read or listen to soft music about an hour before retiring, and try to develop this routine for the same hour each night. Let your mind have a chance to relax and unwind before retiring. Take a brisk walk before going to bed, or just sit a while with your eyes closed and get into a relaxed frame of mind. Don't drink alcohol or coffee before retiring. Warm milk or a hot lemon drink can calm the body and mind and prepare it for a good night's sleep.

Stress Management

Pressure and demands of study or career can cause both physical and mental stress that can affect not only your job performance but your personality. If not controlled, stress can lead to high blood pressure, ulcers, cardiovascular disease, heart problems, and mental breakdowns. Also, the expectation of a stressful event, such as going for a job interview or taking a pre-employment test, can cause as much or more stress than the event itself.

A person with a pleasing personality learns to live with some degree of stress and to manage an overload. Having a positive mental attitude plays a major part in controlling stress. Develop an "I can handle it" attitude, and you will learn to cope successfully with stress so it doesn't drain your energy or hinder your thought process.

Many companies today employ specialists to help their employees learn to handle stress. Techniques range from exercise breaks to at-desk neck and shoulder massages to soft music and humor. John Cleese of Monty Python fame built an entire business around producing comedy-charged industrial videos designed to relieve the stress of employee training.

To manage stress in your work life, which can contribute to relaxation and self-confidence and aid in developing a pleasing personality, try the following:

- Take relaxation breaks during the day to quietly let your mind and body recharge itself.

- Find a quiet place to meditate.

- Develop a hobby to offer a change of pace from your work.

- Take time for stretching and breathing exercises during the day.
- Vary your tasks or environment for short periods daily.

Some stress in your life can be good. It can get you going and offer challenges. Too much stress can be harmful. Learn to develop a happy medium in dealing with stress.

Positive Self-Image

Few people are as attractive or gifted as they wish they could be. Most of us have physical or emotional scars or flaws. You can either ignore them or overcome them.

It is common to read about or see on television an example of someone with a serious impediment who has gone on to become a winner in one way or another. Ray Patterson, though blind, is a champion American bicycle racer, racing tandem four times in the Tour de France. Frank Church was told by doctors that he had "terminal cancer" when he was 23, but went on to become a US senator and lived to the age of 59. Her leg crushed in an auto accident, Cheryl Prewitt of Mississippi was told she would never walk again, but her faith and determination helped her not only to walk but to win the Miss America title in 1980. Dyslexia didn't stop actor Tom Cruise. He overcame it, becoming a million-dollar superstar and "Top Gun."

A learning disability didn't stop some of the most successful men in history. Among other prominent dyslexics are Thomas Edison, Albert Einstein, Nelson A. Rockefeller, General George S. Patton, President Woodrow Wilson, and Hans Christian Andersen.

Some deterrents can be limiting, others can be overcome. No matter if you have a physical issue or if you were born into poverty and there are no role models of achievers in your family, don't label yourself by any of that. Don't falsely identify yourself as having a debilitating problem. Use positive thinking to fight and give yourself a better self-image, which is a key to developing and projecting a pleasing personality and creating the positive energy you need to win, in life and career.

Positive Associations

Associate with people who have positive attitudes. Shun those who complain and have depressing outlooks on life and work. You won't develop or project a winning, positive personality if you don't stay away from naysayers, doom mongers, and constant complainers.

Negativism can be contagious, like any disease. Stay mentally and physically healthy by avoiding those who speak negatively. Make friends with those who have cheerful, optimistic, positive attitudes that can make you feel upbeat, that make you feel more vital, positive, and happy to be alive.

Cheerfulness

Being cheerful costs nothing and pays high dividends. It reflects a positive mental attitude, confident self-image, and a healthy mind and body. It also is one of the most contagious of good character qualities. Most everyone responds favorably to cheerful people and like being around them.

I once observed an associate at work at his desk. He always maintained a rapt attention to his work and I knew him to be someone who went the extra mile for his employer and his fellow workers. What I began to notice after a while that impressed me most was how he dealt with his coworkers and managers. When they came to speak with him at his desk, he stopped his work and always smiled, then spoke in a cheerful, pleasing way.

One day, I asked someone in the office about this pattern I had noticed. My coworker replied, "Tom is a helpful person, and he's habitually cheerful. People always leave his desk with a smile on their face."

Making others feel better by projecting a little cheerfulness. What a simple, painless thing to do.

But how few people practice this positive habit that not only caps a positive personality but brings others around to your side.

This list of qualities to have a positive personality may appear to be rather formidable. But you probably already possess many, if not most, of them. It may only be a matter of bringing out the capabilities already within you.

As part of your preparation for a career, check yourself carefully against the factors on the list. Determine which qualities you lack and which need strengthening, then begin at once to develop those qualities you don't possess.

You need as many of the ingredients of a positive personality as you can possess to market your personal services successfully. You have no reason to expect your services to yield more than they are worth. Make them be worth more by beginning now to develop a well-rounded, success-oriented positive personality.

MAJOR FACTORS OF A *NEGATIVE* PERSONALITY

On the other side of the coin, there are negative personality traits that are roadblocks to success and happiness. It may be as helpful to consider them as it is to identify the factors that make up a positive personality.

Analyze and check yourself carefully against this list to make sure you are not unconsciously carrying around with you an atmosphere that causes people to dislike you:

- *Disloyalty.* People who lack loyalty are poverty stricken, regardless of their other qualities or worldly possessions. They cannot possibly market their personal services effectively because the market for those services will play out as soon as that quality is disclosed.

- *Dishonesty.* This trait is the keystone to the arch of character, and without sound character, no one can market his or her services effectively or successfully.

- *Greed.* A person cursed by greed is always disliked, and greed can't be kept undercover. It is bound to assert itself so clearly that others will shun whoever reflects it.

- *Envy and hatred.* These traits make a pleasing personality impossible. The person who hates people will in turn be hated, regardless of company manners or attempts to cover those disagreeable traits.

- *Jealousy.* This is a mild form of insanity that is fatal to a pleasing personality; it arouses antagonism, and no one likes a jealous person.

- **Anger.** Whether passive or active, anger puts off people and they avoid angry people.
- **Fear.** Fear repels people. It never attracts anything except more fear.
- **Revenge.** A spiteful, revengeful person is repugnant to everyone.
- **Faultfinding.** People who are in the habit of finding fault with others or with conditions aren't pleasing or likable. They might more profitably spend their time looking within themselves for faults.
- **Peddling scandal.** People may listen to gossip because they can't avoid it, but they won't like the person who spreads it.
- **Uncontrolled enthusiasm.** Too much enthusiasm is as bad as none. To be effective, it must be controlled and directed.
- **Evasiveness.** An untruthful person is persona non grata in every household and in every place of business. Lying destroys confidence and sets up an antagonistic environment.
- **Excuses.** Escaping responsibility for mistakes is never pleasing. It's far better to assume responsibility for mistakes you don't make than to form the habit of trying to place responsibility for mistakes on others.
- **Exaggeration.** It's better to understate a truth than to overstate it. Exaggeration causes loss of confidence.
- **Egotism.** Uncontrolled egotism is one of the most

damaging personality traits. There is only one form of acceptable egotism: the habit of expressing your ideas in helpful deeds rather than in words.

- **Self-confidence** is one of the most desirable and necessary traits, but it must be controlled and directed to definite ends, through methods that don't antagonize others. All forms of **self-praise** are easily recognized as evidence of an inferiority complex.

- **Obstinacy.** A person who is obstinate, stubborn, and self-willed is never pleasing. A certain amount of determination and the ability to stand by one's opinions are, of course, essential. But these qualities should not become a blanket policy.

- **Selfishness.** No one likes a selfish person. This trait attracts opposition in every conceivable form.

These are certainly not all of the negative personality traits a person can have, but they are, on the whole, the ones that do the most damage. Be merciless with yourself when you check yourself against the list, remembering that an enemy discovered is an enemy half-conquered.

Keep this thought clearly in mind and be your own severest critic. Remember that a positive personality is a self-acquired asset and calls for self-control and a willingness to change destructive habits.

You establish the limitations of your life through your personal conduct. Just as surely as a criminal is in prison because of conduct reflecting a very negative personality, so are you where you are today and will be tomorrow because of your personality as reflected through your conduct.

Bear in mind these two important statements:

1. A positive personality helps you to market your personal services effectively.

2. Sound character helps you keep your services marketed permanently.

TAKE ACTION

1. Do you have a positive personality? Take time now to go back to the beginning of this chapter. Consider each of the qualities that go into building a pleasing, positive personality. How do you score on each?

2. Are you weak in any of the qualities? If so, give some thought to how you can overcome that weakness and score higher in those qualities of character. It may not be easy, and probably will require a great deal of personal honesty to admit a weakness, but consider that weakness is an enemy, and remember that an enemy discovered is an enemy half-conquered.

3. How do you score on the checklist of traits that make up a negative personality? Are there traits on the list that you possess? How can you

rid yourself of these pitfalls toward achieving a positive, pleasing personality that radiates success and invites the cooperation of others?

9

CREATING YOUR INDIVIDUAL IMPRESSION

There is no other road to genius than through voluntary self-effort.

MAKE YOUR INDIVIDUALITY WORK FOR YOU

All of us carry within ourselves what is known as an individual atmosphere, or impression. This atmosphere is the sum total of our positive personality factors *and* our negative personality factors.

Every workplace has a distinctive atmosphere made up of the combined personalities of the employees. Someone with a pleasing personality or impression can color the workplace atmosphere so much that the entire place is pleasant. On the other hand, someone who has a negative nature and personality can influence the atmosphere so that it becomes a miserable place to work.

Remember that the impression you have of others contributes to the atmosphere of your home and your place of business. Every home carries an atmosphere that clearly indicates whether there is harmony or friction within, and the same is true about a place of business.

A positive atmosphere or culture, while intangible, is one of the greatest assets any business can have. And it may be had only through a combination of positive individual personalities.

People who carry a grouch into their place of employment do almost as much damage to their coworkers and the business as might be done if poison were placed in the drinking water. Employers who understand this principle watch very carefully to see that only cooperative people work in their establishment.

HARMONIOUS COOPERATION

Success is achieved through power, and power is developed through organized and intelligently directed knowledge, which calls for cooperation. In any well-managed business, there is a sense of camaraderie and loyalty among the employees—a spirit of *harmonious* cooperation. You can't market yourself effectively unless you understand and apply this principle.

Note that I have emphasized the word *harmonious,* because cooperation must be more than tentative. It must be real and based on synchronization. This applies to business owners as well as managers and employees. The public expects and demands efficient and pleasant service.

Andrew Carnegie said that the *inability to cooperate stood at the head of the list of the causes of failure.* Moreover, he said he would not tolerate a lack of cooperation no matter how well-equipped a person might be otherwise—because anyone who won't cooperate with others or doesn't gain cooperation from others is a disturbing element whose influence spreads with disastrous results.

Conversely, he declared, a person who cooperates with others and who can induce others to cooperate with him or her is a powerful and positive influence on the entire workforce.

Mr. Carnegie's view may seem harsh. But it's not. It's merely practical, for it has been proven that only one fault-finder in an organization of a thousand people can affect the mental attitude of everyone, thereby creating friction and dissatisfaction throughout.

SELF-PROMOTION AND CONFIDENCE TO SUCCEED

One day Andrew Carnegie sent me to call on Henry Ford. "You want to watch this man Ford," said Carnegie, "for one day he is going to dominate the motor industry in America."

So I went to Detroit in 1908 and met Ford for the first time. My first reaction was to wonder how such a judge of men as Andrew Carnegie could have been so mistaken in his estimation of the president of the Ford Motor Company.

Then, year by year, I watched Ford climb to the top of his field, and behind his stupendous achievement I observed highly organized, systematic, and effective "promotion."

Perhaps no one ever connected with the Ford promotion was of greater service to him than W.J. Cameron, who saw to it that the Ford company interests were never neglected in the eyes of the public. Dozens of other auto manufacturers have risen only to crumble like mushrooms because they didn't have the foresight to surround themselves with promotion experts like Cameron. A notable exception is Lee Iacocca, a promotion genius. He started working at Ford Motor Company, was instrumental in the creation of the Ford Mustang, then worked for Chrysler Corporation and is credited with saving the company from bankruptcy.

By "promotion experts," I don't mean advertising executives. Promotion is one thing, and advertising is something entirely different. Lee Iacocca promoted himself into becoming not only one of the country's highest paid executives, but also one of its most admired men. Many suggested he run for President of the United States.

PROMOTION MEANING

Promotion, the sort I'm referencing, is the art of keeping an individual favorably sold to the public all the time.

Ivy Lee was one of the greatest promotion—or public relations—men of his time. He's the one who kept John D. Rockefeller's name before the public continuously in a favorable light. Lee seldom worked through paid publicity. He preferred free space in the newspapers and other forms of more efficient promotion for keeping his clients properly sold to the public.

While some people criticized Rockefeller for what became a monopoly in the oil industry, others praised him for his generous contributions to philanthropic causes. He spent tens of millions of dollars over his lifetime helping establish YMCAs, the Anti-Saloon League, and the General Education Board; he founded a medical research institute known as Rockefeller University in New York City, and he founded the University of Chicago. He also established the Rockefeller Foundation to promote public health and to further research in the medical, natural, and social sciences. His philanthropic donations totaled more than $540 million in his lifetime and continue to fund worthy humanitarian efforts through The Rockefeller Foundation.

While I was publishing the *Golden Rule Magazine,* I wrote an editorial praising the work of his son, John D. Rockefeller, Jr., who continued his father's philanthropic work. I singled out his fine humanitarian work in going to Colorado to settle the famous coal strike in 1919. Almost before the print dried on my article, I received a wire from Ivy Lee inviting me to visit him in New York. When I arrived, he got down to business without ceremonies, offering me $10,000 a year to join his staff and write similar editorials about other clients of his. That was big money in those days.

Promotion, or PR, experts earn and receive big money because they recognize and have the good sense to use the forces needed to further the interests of their clients. I declined the Ivy Lee offer, but I often regretted the decision; for I came to realize that a few years of schooling under that promotional genius would have been worth many times the sum he offered me to work for him.

John D. Rockefeller Jr. gave almost as much money to philanthropic causes as his father had, $537 million.[10] Among his most notable philanthropies was funding the restoration of colonial Williamsburg, Virginia, and he donated the site for the United Nations headquarters in New York City. He founded and helped plan Rockefeller Center in New York and his son, John D. Rockefeller III, has carried on the family's philanthropic tradition by supporting the Rockefeller Center for the Performing Arts and the United Negro College Fund. Other members of the family also have spent much of their time, energy, and fortunes in philanthropy and public service. Of note, the Rockefeller Philanthropy Advisors website states:

> Also, while the Rockefeller spirit of entrepreneurship has informed their business practices and their giving, they do not operate their nonprofit organizations as though they were businesses. In philanthropy, it is important to engage both the heart and the mind, and so to become personally involved in thoughtful and reflective giving. The impact and continuity of the Rockefeller family's philanthropy draws on four important forces:
>
> Thoughtful transmittal of values, including obligation, opportunity, collaboration and personal investment, through family traditions and organized meetings;
>
> Consistent adherence to a long-term perspective that focuses on root causes, understanding the time horizon and balancing patience with accountability;
>
> Genuine confidence in the nonprofit sector to creatively solve problems that neither government nor business can address through strong and sustainable organizations; and
>
> Clear understanding of how organizations thrive, including the role of operating support, governance vs. management and shared decision-making.
>
> These principles and practices, now reaching the seventh generation of Rockefellers, with more than 150 descendants of John D. Rockefeller Sr.,

have transformed the landscape of philanthropy over the last century—and form a solid platform for continued innovation in giving.

US President Theodore Roosevelt received the benefit of promotion another way. When Teddy returned from a safari in Africa, just after he left the White House in 1909, he made his first public appearance at Madison Square Garden. Before he would agree to appear, he arranged for nearly 1,000 paid applauders to be scattered throughout the audience and applaud his entrance. This was not the first time such people were used at public events. Some of the great pianists, violinists, and opera singers of the past have hired "clackers," people who applaud and cheer to praise a performer or rival jeers and hoot-calls to drive a performer from the stage, depending on the intention of their employer.

At Teddy Roosevelt's arrival in Madison Square Garden, his paid hand-clappers made the huge stadium ring with their enthusiasm for more than 15 minutes. The audience went wild, turning the occasion into a tremendous ovation for the American hero. The next morning, New York newspaper headlines and photos gave Roosevelt a million dollars' worth of free promotion.

Splendid! He understood and made intelligent use of personal promotion.

Today, rock stars, sports celebrities, and movie and television stars all have PR managers to sell them to the public—as do giant corporations.

SELL YOURSELF TO ACHIEVE YOUR GOAL

One of our key duties in life is to sell our way to some definite goal. But, unfortunately, not all of us are efficient salespeople. Therefore, most of us need the services of experienced promotion experts who assume the responsibility of keeping us steadily and favorably before the public.

At one time, an enterprising young Chicago lawyer by the name of Paul Harris conceived a brilliant way of circumventing the rule that prevented lawyers from advertising. He gathered around him 30 or so of his business friends and organized the first Rotary Club. The idea was to promote himself into a variety of contacts who could conceivably be converted into clients as the result of his personal relationship with them once a week. The Rotary Club movement spread worldwide and became an international power for good, far exceeding Harris' expectations.

If you wish to get ahead in the world, you must find ways and means to bring yourself to the attention of people who need whatever you have to offer them. Building a better mousetrap than someone else will avail nothing without sound, intense, and continuous sales promotion.

Actors wait hungrily for casting calls in Hollywood, trying to sell their talents. Once in a blue moon, a studio will discover a new actor or actress and promote them to the top, but the blue moons don't rise very often.

Rather than waiting to be discovered, it's better to search until you find the person best-equipped to market the sort of services you have to offer. Then give that person a good block of stock in yourself and say, "Go ahead, promote me!"

While meeting an editor of a syndicated service with my manager negotiating for the sale of some of my works, he told me that everyone in the literary field reached the top through clever promotion. He mentioned in particular Dr. Frank Crane, who used to write a daily column for the newspapers.

"When Doctor Crane first came to us," said this distinguished editor, "he was peddling his stuff here and there, wherever he could get a country weekly newspaper to buy it, not earning enough to keep him and his family."

When Dr. Crane died, he was being paid a yearly income of more than $75,000 (today that would be about $300,000), all of his income coming from the sale of his column, marketed by a promotion expert.

Today writers can both write books and lecture about them, being their own PR agents. Others such as movie, television, and music performers go on promotional tours arranged by their studios or recording companies. They make appearances on television and radio talk shows to promote themselves and their latest show or record. All are refined methods of self-promotion.

WAKE UP CALL

I spent a quarter of a century organizing the philosophy of individual achievement. I wrote into that philosophy all that had been retrieved from the experiences of such men as Andrew Carnegie, Henry Ford, Thomas A. Edison, and others of their type. Yet I found myself outmoded by people who wrote books they had thrown together overnight, as far as financial income was concerned.

I finally awakened to myself. I placed myself under the management of my wife, and duty impels me to admit that I accomplished more in the way of recognition during the first year of her management than I had during all my previous years while serving as my own manager.

It is our duty and responsibility to provide ourselves with whatever form of promotion is needed to help us attain success in our chosen calling. But self-advancement cannot be built on bluff, fear, or flattery!

Success in life demands sterner stuff than these. Mere words and fine platitudes will never take the place of a practical plan doggedly put into action.

The most that can be said of flattery is that it is sometimes a cheap psychological trick that charlatans and dishonest people use to lull people into a state of carelessness while they pick their pockets. Flattery is the top tool of all "con men." The human ego is a tricky piece of mental equipment. It needs constant protection against all forms of flattery, which the ego responds to readily.

It is said that John W. Davis was paid an enormous sum annually by the J.P. Morgan banking firm, not for what he told the members of the firm they could do, but for what he told them they couldn't do. He was the official "no man" of the firm, and he did no flattering to "win and influence" the Morgan partners. Astute businessmen prefer cold facts to flattery.

Truly great business leaders do not depend on flattery to get results. They have a better formula. Andrew Carnegie did not flatter Charles M. Schwab, who started out as a stake driver in Carnegie's steelworks and rose to become president of the Carnegie Steel Company and then the first president of the U.S.

Steel Corporation. Carnegie got more dependable results by paying Schwab as high as a million dollars a year for his brains and his personality, *for demanding loyalty from his workers and getting it!* Schwab did this primarily by spreading enthusiasm among Carnegie employees, through showing appreciation of their efforts and encouraging them.

SELL YOURSELF SUCCESSFULLY

Life is made up of situations and circumstances calling for decisions to be made. People who negotiate their way through life successfully learn to use a yes or a no each in its proper place.

Abraham Lincoln kept bitter enemies as members of his presidential cabinet because he needed their frank analysis and criticism. Woodrow Wilson ousted cabinet members who did not agree with him. The difference in the records of the two US Presidents is very great and will probably become greater with time.

How far would a military man get in warfare if soldiers were managed by flattery? And how far do you think flattery would get you with most police officers and taxi drivers?

Individuals who make themselves indispensable to others by rendering more service and better service than they are paid to render will accomplish more permanent results of a desirable nature than they could accomplish with all the flattery in the world.

To sell your way through life successfully, look around you and see what useful service you can render to as many people as possible. Make yourself valuable to others, and you won't need flattery to win people. Moreover, they will remain loyal because you are sincere.

To be well-liked gives you great advantages in many substantial ways. A pleasing personality is worth much, but such a personality is not developed through words of flattery that mean nothing.

A pleasing personality consists of 26 different characteristics that can be developed, as outlined in Chapter 8. Master them and make them your own to attract and keep friends and customers.

There are practical and tried rules for making good impressions that attract people to you. These are not the rules used to gain temporary advantages over people. These are rules gleaned from the lifework of Abraham Lincoln, Benjamin Franklin, Thomas Paine, Thomas Jefferson, Samuel Adams, Richard Henry Lee, George Washington, and half a hundred other truly great people who laid the very foundation of this great country.

These are the rules used also by the most successful business and industrial leaders the country has produced, from Andrew Carnegie and Thomas A. Edison to today's most successful men such as Sam Walton of Walmart and Bill Gates of Microsoft.

There are sound and commendable ways of winning friends and influencing people through appeal based on some combination of the ten basic motives which follow. Every move, every act, and every thought of every human being of sound body and mind who has reached the age of reason is influenced by one or more of the ten basic motives.

Study each of the following *ten basic motives* carefully and learn how to influence people by a genuine appeal to natural motives. This way you will experience no resentment from those whom you influence.

THE TEN BASIC MOTIVES THAT INSPIRE ALL VOLUNTARY ACTION

1. ***Self-Preservation.*** The self-preservation motive was originally used to defend early people against enemies. Now it relates to the desire for material wealth and the struggle for preservation against want and fear. In today's world, it is manifest as the desire for economic security.

2. ***Love.*** The greatest of all motives is love. Love is a psychic force related to the spiritual side of humans. There are three different attitudes in the expression of someone's love: 1) a labor of love, work you enjoy doing and brings forth your best creative effort; 2) a love of truth or principle—the love of an ideal leading to spiritual enlightenment and knowledge; 3) love of another person.

3. ***Fear.*** There are seven basic fears: 1) fear of poverty, 2) fear of ill health, 3) fear of criticism, 4) fear of the loss of love of friends and relatives, 5) fear of old age, 6) fear of the loss of liberty, and 7) fear of death.

4. ***Sex.*** Sex is the physical complement of love. The emotion of sex can be sublimated and diverted in such a way that it becomes a truly irresistible

power for action behind a person's goal in life. (Andrew Carnegie said, "There has never yet been born a great leader in any form of human endeavor who did not attain his leadership through the mastering and direction of the power generated by the great emotions of love and sex!")

5. *Life after death.* A desire for perpetual life is closely allied with the desire for self-preservation and it is instinctive in human nature.

6. *Freedom of body and mind.* The basic wish in everyone's heart is the desire to be free and unfettered.

7. *Hate.* Getting angry and holding hatred in our hearts is a waste of mental energy, a dissipation of our psychic force, and an unproductive use of our precious time.

8. *Revenge.* Although the feeling of getting even with someone is basically human, it is utterly wasteful. Revenge builds or improves nothing and no one. Holding a grudge results in a negative mental attitude—the exact opposite of a constructive and positive mental attitude required for success.

9. *Self-expression and recognition.* We should be working harder for the opportunity to express ourselves and to gain public recognition rather than for money.

10. **Material gain.** Desire for material gain is fundamental in human nature. Combine the emotion of love, the emotion of sex, and the desire for material gain or wealth and you have the three motives that make the world go around. But remember, the real good in money is how it's used—not the mere possession of it.

Now I suggest a creed for you to consider adopting concerning material riches:

> I give thanks daily, not for mere riches, but for wisdom to recognize, embrace, and properly use the great abundance of riches I now have at my command. I have no enemies because I injure no one for any cause; rather, I try to benefit all people by teaching them the way to enduring riches. I have more material wealth than I need because I am free from greed and covet only the material things I can use while I live.

By mastering, understanding, and applying the ten basic motives, you can reduce misunderstandings, opposition, and friction. Do this and you will be a great salesperson, no matter what your calling may be. Let me give you an example from my own experience.

At the end of the first year of the Depression, in 1930, I found myself divested of my money and most of my worldly property. People were not interested in books, which I was writing. They were interested in eating. I closed my New York office and moved to Washington, DC, where I planned to remain until the economic storm had passed.

Months stretched out into years, and instead of the Depression passing, it became worse. Finally, I decided not to wait for the end of the business stagnation, but to go on the lecture circuit and work my way back into useful service to others who had also been wounded.

I decided to start in Washington. For this purpose, I needed newspaper space for advertising. The amount of space I required would cost more than $2,000, which I didn't have, neither could I get it from the usual banking sources. I was face to face with a situation similar to what many must sometimes experience. I needed something I had to procure with mere words.

Here, then, is a brief description of exactly what I did and said to surmount my problem. I went to the advertising director of the *Washington Star,* and made my needs known to him. In approaching him, I had two courses available: 1) I could flatter him, telling him what a great newspaper he represented, what a fine record he had made in the World War, and what a great advertising man I believed him to be, and all that sort of piffle. Or, 2) I could lay all my cards on the table and tell him what I wanted, why I wanted it, and why I believed I should get it. I chose the latter approach.

Then I had to decide whether I would disclose to the ad director all the facts, including my financial weakness, or skip over those embarrassing subjects. Again, I chose to rely on frankness and directness. As well as I can remember, here is a word-for-word account of what I said:

"I wish to use the *Washington Star* in an advertising campaign to announce a series of public lectures on the philosophy of individual achievement. The space I require will amount to approximately twenty-five hundred dollars. My problem is in the unpleasant fact that I do not have that amount of money available. I had that amount and more a short time ago, but the Depression consumed it.

"My request for this credit is not based on the usual commercial credit rating. On that basis, I would not be entitled to the credit. My appeal is based on the fact (plenty of evidence of which I am prepared to present to you here and now) that I have devoted a quarter of a century to the study of the principles of individual achievement. During this time, I have had the active cooperation of such men as Andrew Carnegie, Thomas A. Edison, Frank A. Vanderlip, John Wanamaker, and Cyrus H.K. Curtis. These men thought enough of me to give freely of their time and experience over a long period of years, while I was organizing the philosophy of success. The time each gave to me was worth many times the amount of credit I am asking of you. Through their cooperation, I am now prepared to take to the world a philosophy of self-help which all the people of the world badly need.

"If you do not wish to extend to me the credit as a sound business risk, then extend it in the same spirit of helpfulness that these men of affairs gave to me of their time and experience."

The credit was extended to me on my brief statement of my case, with this significant remark from the ad director:

"I don't know what your chances are of paying for the space you want, but I believe I know enough of human nature to understand that you intend to pay for the space. I also believe that any philosophy organized from the life work of such men as Edison and Carnegie is sound and needed at this time. Moreover, I believe anyone to whom these men would devote their priceless time is worthy of much more credit than you seek with the *Star*. Bring in your copy and I will run it. We will talk to the credit manager afterward."

After my lectures were successful and the advertising had been paid for, I called on the ad director again. I asked him to tell me frankly why he extended the credit even though I told him all about my financial weakness and nothing whatsoever of my ability to pay the account.

His reply was illuminating. "I gave you the credit," he said, "because you made no attempt to cover up your financial weakness. You resorted to no subterfuge and did not set your best foot forward first."

How far do you suppose I would have gotten had I appealed to him with anything but frankness?

I believe this same business approach would be as successful today, though much has changed. The old-time salesman carried with him a supply of cigars, good liquor, and interesting stories to entertain his prospective buyers. All these have been supplanted by sophisticated computer graphics and charts that the sales people can paint in the mind of prospective buyers a perfect picture of the merchandise he sells.

APPLY SELF-PROMOTION PRINCIPLES

You may be asking, *How can I apply the principles of self-promotion in this chapter to start a career?* Maybe you haven't yet achieved sufficient knowledge or experience to warrant hiring a PR person to keep your name favorably in front of your employer or the general public. The time for that may come later, after you have achieved some degree of success.

For now, an important first step toward honest and justified self-promotion can be taken by choosing a highly capable and respected person in your personal or work life and demonstrating through your strength of personality and dedication to good, honest work that you are exceptional.

Once you have a person of high regard and influence on your side, you have taken the first step toward successful self-promotion. That person will take the ball from there, speaking favorably on your behalf to others, making them aware of your exceptional qualities.

A good start toward finding someone to recognize your exceptional qualities is to give more and better service than you are paid to give. Be cheerful and loyal. Demonstrate controlled enthusiasm. Soon, people in positions of power will recognize your exceptional qualities and say a "good word" on your behalf to those who can offer you advancement.

Just remember, sincerity and honesty plus hard work will get you favorable promotion. "Buttering up" someone with the obvious intention of conning them into helping promote you will achieve the opposite effect.

In closing this chapter on creating your individual impression, I offer these thoughts: Seek the counsel of people who will tell you the truth about yourself, even if it hurts you to hear it. Mere commendation will not bring the improvement you seek.

Finally, study again and again the Ten Basic Motives that inspire all voluntary action. Control and use of these strongest motives in our human makeup provide the secret to success in life and work. They lead you to a positive means so you can deal harmoniously with others and favorably influence them on your behalf, which is the secret to success in any career.

TAKE ACTION

1. What does self-promotion mean? How does it differ from advertising?

2. Can you think of entertainers, sports figures, television or movie stars who use self-promotion to keep their name favorably before the public? Are any active in philanthropic or public service causes?

3. Are you an effective self-promoter? Do you need a promotion expert to "sell" your services to others?

4. What do you think of people who flatter and agree with everything you say?

5. Read and reread the Ten Basic Motives that inspire all voluntary action. How strong are each of the motives in your life? Are you in control of each of the ten motives? If not, which motives may be excessively strong in your nature or personality? Give thought and effort to bring it under control and more properly and successfully handle those emotions and motives.

6. If you had all the wealth you ever dreamed of having, what would you do with it? If you had "enough," would you still want more?

7. How would you have asked the *Washington Star's* advertising director to give you $2,500 worth of credit?

8. Are you currently worthy self-promotion? If not, how can you achieve the qualities that make you exceptional and worthy of promotion?

9. Who among your friends, teachers, or people you work with could you influence to promote you to others? How would you gain their respect and admiration so they would act favorably on your behalf?

10. Write down the Ten Basic Motives on a sheet of paper. Refer to them often. Consider whether you have all ten of the motives under control. If you don't have any of the motives under control, work toward achieving this goal.

NOTE

10. "John Rockefeller Jr., *Philanthropy Roundtable;* https://www.philanthropyroundtable.org/hall-of-fame/john-rockefeller-jr/; accessed May 29, 2024.

10

SELF-ASSESSMENT ANALYSIS

All people are who they are because of their dominating thoughts and desires.

And now, may I introduce you to one of the greatest of all teachers?

The one person in all the world who can do the most to help you solve your personal problems, whatever they may be!

The one person you can rely on with a faith that will not disappoint you.

The person you can turn to in times of stress and discouragement.

The only person who can give you a direct connection with Infinite Intelligence.

And, as far as you are concerned, the most important person now living!

Who is that person? *Yourself!*

Not the self who frets and fears and complains and lays miseries at the doors of the others—but the "other self" who takes orders only from the power within, and is, therefore, infallible!

PERSONAL INVENTORY SELF-ANALYSIS

Annual self-analysis is essential and over time should reveal a decrease of faults and an increase in virtues. We either go ahead, stand still, or go backward in life. Our objective should be, of course, to go ahead, to keep advancing toward our goals, following our plan leading to success.

Your annual self-assessment should be made at the end of each year, so you can include in your New Year's Resolutions any improvements the analysis indicates should be made. Take this inventory by asking yourself the following questions, and check your answers with the aid of someone who will ensure your answers are accurate:

1. Have I attained the goal I established as my objective for this past year? (You should work with a yearly objective as part of your *definite primary purpose plan*).

2. Did I deliver service of the best possible *quality,* or could I improve any part of this service?

3. Have I delivered service in the greatest possible *quantity?*

4. Has the spirit of my conduct been harmonious and cooperative at all times?

5. Have I permitted the habit of *procrastination* to decrease my efficiency? If so, to what extent?

6. Have I improved my *personality?* If so, in what ways?

7. Was I *persistent* in following my plans through to completion?

8. Have I made *prompt and definite decisions* on all occasions?

9. Did I permit *fear* to decrease my efficiency?

10. Have I been either over-cautious or under-cautious?

11. Has my relationship with my work associates been pleasant or unpleasant? If unpleasant, has the fault been partly or wholly mine?

12. Has my energy lapsed because I lost my *concentration?*

13. Am I consistently open-minded and tolerant?

14. In what way have I *improved* my ability to render service?

15. Have I been *overindulgent* in any of my habits?

16. Have I expressed, either openly or secretly, any form of *egotism?*

17. Has my conduct toward my associates caused them to *respect* me?

18. Have my *decisions* been based on guesswork or accurate analysis and thought?

19. Have I established the *habit of budgeting* my time, expenses, and income?

20. How much time have I devoted to *unprofitable* effort?

21. How can I *re-budget* my time and change my habits to be more efficient?

22. Have I been guilty of any conduct not approved by my *conscious?*

23. Have I provided *more and better service* than I was paid to provide?

24. Have I been *unfair* to anyone? If so, in what way? Did I make it right?

25. If I were the purchaser of my own services for the past year, would I be satisfied with my purchase?

26. Am I in the right vocation? If not, why not?

27. Have the purchasers of my services been satisfied? If not, why not?

28. What is my present rating on the fundamental principles of success? (Make this rating fairly and frankly, and have it checked by someone who is courageous enough to respond accurately.)

PERSONALITY TESTS

Today's access to seemingly limitless information provides knowledge on any topic at any time. In the context of successful career planning, there are specific personality tests that target people struggling with career, relationship, and other life decisions.

A quick internet search produces more than 1 million results for the phrase "personality tests." All boasting to provide insights into the test-taker's behavioral tendencies, preferences, traits, and ultimately reveal a personality "type."

As a people leader, personality tests help you understand how people act and why. It's like learning a secret language that helps everyone get along better at work and in teams. This tool shows how different we are and how those differences can make us stronger together.

When you know people's personality styles, you will find that talking to and working with them is more enjoyable and productive. You will understand people better, which makes for friendlier coworkers. Taking a personality test can change the way you see others—and yourself!

NAPOLEON HILL

(1883-1970)

> **"Remember that your real wealth can be measured not by what you have—but by what you are."**

In 1908, during a particularly down time in the U.S. economy and with no money and no work, Napoleon Hill took a job to write success stories about famous men. Although it would not provide much in the way of income, it offered Hill the opportunity to meet and profile the giants of industry and business—the first of whom was the creator of America's steel industry, multimillionaire Andrew Carnegie, who became Hill's mentor.

Carnegie was so impressed by Hill's perceptive mind that following their three-hour interview, he invited Hill to spend the weekend at his estate so they could continue the discussion. During the course of the next two days, Carnegie told Hill that he believed any person could achieve greatness if they understood the philosophy of success and the steps required to achieve it. "It's a shame," he said, "that each new generation must find the way to success by trial and error when the principles are really clear-cut."

Carnegie went on to explain his theory that this knowledge could be gained by interviewing those who had achieved greatness and then compiling the information and research into a comprehensive set of principles. He believed that it would take at least twenty years, and that the result would be "the world's first philosophy of individual achievement." He offered Hill the challenge—for no more compensation than that Carnegie would make the necessary introductions and cover travel expenses.

It took Hill 29 seconds to accept Carnegie's proposal. Carnegie told him afterward that had it taken him more than sixty seconds to make the decision, he would have withdrawn the offer, for "a man who cannot reach a decision promptly, once he has all the necessary facts, cannot be depended on to carry through any decision he may make."

It was through Napoleon Hill's unwavering dedication that his book, *Think and Grow Rich,* was written and more than 80 million copies have been sold.

CHECK OUT THE
LIVE A LIFE THAT MATTERS SERIES

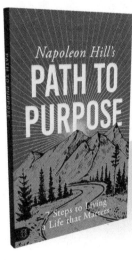

Path to Purpose

7 Steps to
Living a Life that Matters

Achieving Your Goals

The Four Proven
Principles of Success

How to Create a
Motivated Mindset

Stay on the Path to Purpose
and Achieve Your Goals

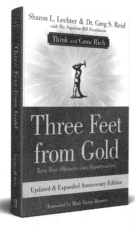

THANK YOU FOR READING THIS BOOK!

If you found any of the information helpful, please take a few minutes and leave a review on the bookselling platform of your choice.

BONUS GIFT!

Don't forget to sign up to try our newsletter and grab your free personal development ebook here:

soundwisdom.com/classics